"Filled with concrete and actionable tips from the *Quick Start Guide* in the beginning to the *Resources and References* at the end—and on every page between—Bill Eddy and Randi Kreger's *Splitting* is quite simply THE absolute MUST resource for those going through a high-conflict divorce and the professionals who support them. I will be keeping a copy on my desk going forward!"

—**Susan Guthrie**, leading divorce attorney and mediator, cofounder of the Mosten Guthrie Academy, and host of *The Divorce & Beyond Podcast*

"This book includes important considerations when planning for physical and emotional safety in court proceedings, particularly when a relationship has been violent and/or abusive. So often, when a person leaves a relationship where their partner has been abusive, the court system becomes the next tool to continue harassment, intimidation, and psychological abuse. My hope is that anyone in our community who feels that there is no way to safely navigate this intimidating process will find this book to be a resourceful and helpful guide."

—**Anna Harper-Guerrero, LMSW**, executive vice president and chief strategy officer at the Emerge Center Against Domestic Abuse in Tucson, AZ

"Parents who find themselves embroiled in high-conflict and court involvement with a co-parent who has a personality disorder face overwhelming challenges to resolve custody disputes and manage their ongoing co-parenting relationship. Bill and Randi not only help readers understand what drives the behaviors of borderline, narcissistic, and antisocial parents, but provide comprehensive and specific advice to help the healthier parent navigate the family court experience and alternatives to formal legal processes when dealing with these individuals. Their comprehensive, step-by-step advice when confronted with a 'persuasive blamer' is a lifeline to parents and professionals alike."

—**Matthew J. Sullivan**, immediate past president of the Association of Family and Conciliation Courts

"Two noted authorities offer eminently practical advice that has stood the test of time. Whether in the process of breaking up, or managing the troubling aftermath of a split, this comprehensive guide will be your lifeline. Chock-full of advice to protect and empower yourself when dealing with a difficult ex. The clear strategies for effectively presenting and defending your position in court are priceless. For your own well-being, and for your children, get this book and keep it handy."

—**Richard A. Warshak, PhD**, author of *Divorce Poison*

"*Splitting* is a practical, concise guide as to what to expect when dealing with a high-conflict person in a divorce context. The authors do not sugarcoat the behaviors that will occur during a divorce involving a high-conflict person. Their charts and management suggestions are direct and easy to process. This volume is useful for anyone engaged in handling family law matters."

—**Retired Judge Christine Goldsmith,**
San Diego Superior Court, family law mediator

"Eddy and Kreger's *Splitting* is the book that those embroiled in difficult family court proceedings will call 'a life saver,' and the book that 'made me realize I'm not alone.' Every family court participant will benefit from their expertise in understanding, managing, preparing, and ultimately succeeding in family court despite an opposing party's scorched-earth tactics."

—**Annette T. Burns**, past president of the Association of Family and Conciliation Courts; fellow of the American Academy of Matrimonial Lawyers; attorney and family law certified specialist; and coauthor of *BIFF for Coparent Communication*

"For anyone targeted by a 'persuasive blamer,' this is a must-read. You will learn strategies for responding to blamers' predictable and often effective court tactics. Recognizing the importance of safety planning where there is risk of domestic violence, the authors make a compelling case for mediation given how the adversarial family court system can escalate aggression. Every family lawyer should include a copy of this book with their initial consult!"

—**Hilary A. Linton, JD, LLM**, award-winning family lawyer, mediator, and arbitrator in Toronto, ON, Canada; who trains professionals how to assess and manage domestic violence

# Praise for the first edition:

"*Splitting* provides concise, clear, and invaluable advice for strategically navigating a divorce from someone who has narcissistic personality disorder (NPD) or borderline personality disorder (BPD). Following the suggestions laid out in this book will greatly increase the readers' odds of having a successful marital dissolution under these difficult circumstances."

> —**Susan Pease Gadoua, LCSW**, founder and executive director of the Transition Institute of Marin, and author of *Contemplating Divorce* and *Stronger Day by Day*

# splitting

SECOND EDITION

Protecting Yourself While **Divorcing**
Someone with **Borderline** or
Narcissistic Personality Disorder

Bill Eddy, LCSW, JD
Randi Kreger

New Harbinger Publications, Inc.

## Publisher's Note

New Harbinger Publications is an employee-owned company

NEW HARBINGER PUBLICATIONS is a registered trademark of New Harbinger Publications, Inc.

Copyright © 2021 by Bill Eddy and Randi Kreger
New Harbinger Publications, Inc.
5720 Shattuck Avenue
Oakland, CA 94609
www.newharbinger.com

Cover design by Amy Shoup

Acquired by Jennye Garibaldi

Edited by Nelda Street

Library of Congress Cataloging-in-Publication Data on file

Printed in the United States of America

26    25    24

10    9    8    7    6    5

# splitting

SECOND EDITION

# Contents

# PART 3: **Succeeding Out of Court**

# Quick-Start Guide

Since a lot can happen suddenly and big mistakes can be made when you are separating or divorcing any difficult person, we start here with some important quick tips:

1. **PLAN:** Develop an emergency plan. Your partner could assault or evict you at any time. Figure out a safe place to go, get some ready cash, and think about who can help you on short notice. Copy important records and keep them in a safe place. (See chapter 5.)

2. **WRITE:** As soon as possible after problems and events between you and your partner (and others) occur, write down accurate details that could become issues in court. Keep a journal or other written record of anything pertinent. If other people were present, write down their names. Save email and text-message correspondence in a safe place, especially copies of hostile, harassing, and controversial exchanges. (See chapter 5.)

3. **COMMUNICATE:** Communicate very carefully and respectfully with your partner, because anything may be introduced into evidence. Make any texts and emails, whether initiated by you or in response to your partner, brief, informative, friendly, and firm (BIFF; see chapter 4). This is especially true if your partner's texts and emails are hostile.

4. **CHILDREN:** Protect your children from conflicts between you and your partner. Don't say anything against your partner in front of the children, no matter how provoked you might be, because anything could become evidence. Avoid:

   - Asking your children questions about the other parent

   - Discussing court with your children or within their hearing

   - Asking your children to compare you and your partner

   - Giving your children choices between their two parents

   - Exposing your children to your negative emotions

5. **SELF-PROTECTION:** Be aware of the risks of violence, false allegations, being evicted from your own home, getting served with papers at work, assets getting hidden, and rumors being spread. Avoid setups for violent confrontations, such as physically fighting over papers, or pushing and shoving. Indicate that you want to settle issues out of court to keep things calm, but always be prepared for the realistic possibility of court. (See chapters 4, 5, 13, and 14.)

6. **PROFESSIONAL HELP:** Consult with or hire a therapist to help you understand your partner's behavior, anticipate problems, deal with your emotions around the divorce or separation, and learn about yourself. (See chapter 5.) Consult with or hire a lawyer with good communication skills and prepare with them for predictable crises and accusations. (See chapters 6 and 8.)

7. **SOCIAL MEDIA:** Stop using Facebook, Twitter, and any other publicly accessible online social networking account that can be used against you someday. Make sure your passwords are secure. Make sure that what you want to keep private, such as letters or lists, is kept private. You should not delete any electronically stored information (it may be legally required at court someday), but you should keep it in a secure place. It may be a good idea to put all communications and documents on a thumb drive, so they're not on your computer hard drive and vulnerable to hacking.

8. **SUPPORT PEOPLE:** Tell your family and friends what to expect, how to respond, how they can help, and how to avoid splitting either of you into being viewed as all good or all bad. (See chapter 5 and the letters to professionals, family, and friends mentioned in Resources.)

9. **DON'T LABEL YOUR PARTNER:** Avoid telling your spouse or co-parent (and anyone who talks to them) that you believe he or she has a personality disorder. This always backfires personally, as well as in future negotiations and in court. This can make you look very bad. It's tempting, but don't do it! (See chapter 14.)

10. **ENCOURAGING WORDS:** Give yourself some encouraging words as you go through this process. Those who are prepared, as described in this book, generally do well and often grow stronger. Many have told us that they were proud of the way they managed this difficult period.

Begin all of these steps right away, even before separating, if possible. If your partner is a potential "persuasive blamer" (see chapter 3), there's a risk that the blamer might use anything you do:

- As an excuse for abuse or violence

- To spread rumors against you

- To publicly humiliate you

- As the basis for allegations and decisions against you in family court and possibly other courts

# Introduction to the
# Second Edition

Sad to say, nothing fundamental has changed about the psychological and legal information that you need since the first edition of this book was published by New Harbinger in 2011. However, there have been many minor changes that are addressed in this second edition, plus significant information about antisocial personalities and a new chapter, "Presenting Your Case."

Psychologically, personality disorders continue to increase in society and in family courts. The fifth edition of the *Diagnostic and Statistical Manual of the American Psychiatric Association* (the *DSM-5*) was published in 2013, so there are relevant updates in this book. The *DSM-5* states that approximately 15 percent of adults in the United States meet the criteria for a personality disorder (APA, 2013, 646), which is equal to or greater than the percentage of adults with a substance use disorder. With the increased reliance on the internet for information, everyone has more awareness of these disorders now, but much of it is incorrect.

In addition to difficult divorces with borderline and narcissistic personalities, we are also seeing more cases involving antisocial personality disorder. While this personality was mentioned in the first edition, there is much more information about the dynamics of this disorder in this edition.

Legally, family courts have been paying much more attention to domestic violence, parental alienation, and child support enforcement. Family courts have also been dealing with more LGBTQ cases, primarily in regard to parenting disputes. The result is many more laws addressing these issues, but a wide disparity of outcomes depending on one's state and local court system.

A larger percentage of today's court hearings are about conflicts over parenting time with the children, which are involving more people with personality disorders. Yet, the courts are still not good at managing behavior problems or understanding the blaming behavior of people with high-conflict personality disorders. Their abusive behavior is often excused and sometimes the blame is shifted to a reasonable parent based on false allegations. To deal with this continuing problem, more strategies for presenting accurate information in court have been added to the book, especially in chapters 7, "Abuse, Alienation, and False Allegations," and chapter 14, "Presenting Your Case."

More people are representing themselves in family courts than ever before, so that courts have adopted more procedures to help them. However, judges and lawyers also privately believe that a significant percentage of self-representing parties have high-conflict personalities, so that you have to be careful that you present yourself as a reasonable person. This makes it even more important that you spend a day observing in your courthouse, that you learn the local rules, and that you at least consult with a lawyer. We still recommend that you retain a lawyer if you are going to a court hearing against someone with one of these confusing and blaming disorders.

Another development is that mediation is being used more. Many court systems require you to try mediation first before coming to court about a parenting matter. This is good news, as you may be able to keep things calmer in mediation or other forms of negotiation, such as collaborative divorce. Yet you still need to be prepared for court because of the all-or-nothing thinking a former spouse or partner may have.

Other good news is that there are more lawyers, judges, mediators, and counselors who realize that people with borderline, narcissistic, and antisocial personality disorders exist and are showing up in high-conflict divorce and child custody disputes. The bad news is that a majority of professionals still do not understand this and are easily misled, confused, or downright unhelpful. There is more hope if you shop around, but you may need to be more persistent to find the good ones.

Ten years ago, Bill's New Ways for Families® method of teaching parents decision-making and communication skills was just getting started. We are pleased to say that several court systems have been ordering this method in the United States and Canada, either as short-term counseling or as an online program, to get parents on the same page and working together for the best interests of the children. Bill has trained counselors in over thirty cities in this method. Many cases have been resolved out of court after using New Ways for Families that previously would have ended up in court hearings over months or years.

Lastly, there is the long-term impact of the coronavirus and the reduced economy on divorce and custody disputes. These will most likely cause more use of mediation and other out-of-court negotiation methods to save time and money and reduce reliance on smaller court budgets. In court, there will be more use of electronic systems for filing papers and holding hearings by telephone or video conferencing. But the predictable problems of handling a case with a difficult partner in the family court system are likely to remain fundamentally the same.

—Bill Eddy and Randi Kreger

# PART 1

# Preparing for a Difficult Divorce

# Chapter 1

# Preparing Yourself

*Sarah was scared. She didn't know what to expect. For three years, Sam had verbally abused her, constantly blamed her, and sometimes even hit her. She was considering separating from him, but she still loved him and hoped it could work out somehow for them to be happy together, as they used to be. Then again, she wondered,* If I actually separate from him, would he come after me and really hurt me? Or would he respect me and try to treat me better?

*Thomas's wife, Tammy, had extreme mood swings, from extremely demanding to overwhelmingly loving—all in the same hour!—and was very inconsistent with their daughter. Thomas worked hard at his job, but Tammy sometimes showed up at his workplace and claimed he was hiding money. Thomas didn't know what his wife would do if he pursued a divorce. Tammy had hinted that she would say he abused their daughter if he ever abandoned her. He wondered,* Would the court believe me—or her? Should I get a lawyer or try to represent myself?

# Personalities in Difficult Divorces

These days, handling difficult divorces is less about legal issues and more about difficult personalities. Sarah and Thomas have partners who may have borderline personality disorder (BPD) or narcissistic personality disorder (NPD) or both. If you can relate to the types of issues they are facing, or other issues in a difficult divorce, this book is for you—whether or not your partner has one of these disorders and regardless of where you are in the separation or divorce process (before, during, or after).

We have learned that these personalities, in particular, can affect every step of the legal process. Most books on divorce don't explain this. We will show you how to protect yourself with this knowledge so that you don't overreact or just give up. We will brief you on what to expect and offer many strategies for what you can do, following Sarah's and Thomas's examples along the way.

# Predictable Patterns

Sarah and Thomas each face a double dose of fear:

- Fear of separating from a partner whose extreme behaviors reflect those of someone with BPD or NPD (or just traits without a full disorder, so we will refer to them as simply BPs and NPs)

- Fear of a family court system that seems totally confusing and unpredictable

If you have these fears, you're not alone. Though they are very common and familiar to millions of people around the world, people rarely discuss them openly. We want you to know that the behavior patterns of people with BP and NP traits in separation and divorce are highly predictable—and are not your fault. We've seen them hundreds of times. In this book we will predict many of the problems you may face. You might be shocked at how typical your partner's behaviors are and wonder, *Do these authors know my husband? Have they met my wife?* (We hear this all the time.)

It's not that we have any special abilities. It's that people with these types of personalities have a narrow range of behaviors, especially under stress. Most people don't see these patterns, but once you know what to look for, you will be surprised at how well you can predict the ups and downs and the problems your spouse will display in the months ahead. The better you can predict future behavior, the better prepared you will be. Of course, this doesn't make it easy. So we have filled this book with tips for coping with a potentially borderline or narcissistic partner—or any partner—while going through the process of your separation or divorce.

# For Married or Unmarried Couples

It doesn't matter whether you are married or no longer married, or have never married; the personality dynamics, legal issues, and responses we describe are very similar whatever your marital status. Therefore, we use the term "divorce" broadly to apply to married and unmarried couples and to address issues at the time of separation, in family court, and out of court. We refer to your "partner" broadly to mean the person with whom you are or were married, share or shared a residence, share a child, or any combination of these situations.

# Family Court

Over the past few decades, the family court system has received more and more public attention as the number of high-conflict divorces has increased. There are certainly enough horror stories and criticisms to make anyone going through a divorce very nervous. However, family court and legal professionals can also be highly predictable, especially in high-conflict cases with BP or NP partners involved. There are predictable strategies to deal with them as well.

Of course, we make no guarantees. You must use your own judgment and get lots of advice from your local attorney, therapist, and other advisers. We are offering general principles that we have seen work in family courts around the United States, Canada, and other countries. Surprisingly, we get feedback from people around the world describing the same patterns of personality-based behavior and the same patterns of problems in their family courts.

## Splitting

The biggest pattern to prepare for is "splitting." This book's title, *Splitting*, has a double meaning. The first is obvious: splitting up. The second meaning refers to a defense mechanism universally seen in people with BPD and NPD. It means unconsciously seeing people as either all good or all bad, an extreme way of coping with confusion, anxiety, and mixed feelings. Splitting is especially prevalent under stress, particularly the stress of breaking up with someone the partner with BPD or NPD views as critical to his or her emotional survival. People who split in this manner put their partners on pedestals and then knock them down.

Perhaps you are familiar with this pattern. In the beginning of your relationship, your partner may have idolized you, and vice versa. Now that you're involved in a separation and divorce, your partner sees you as all bad to the extreme and may act abusively or make numerous false statements. This is an

unconscious effort to cope with the emotions of loss of attachment to you (typical of people with BP traits), loss of an inflated
self-image (typical of people with NP traits), and loss of control
(typical of both). This is true whether it is you or your partner
initiating the separation.

Because of this unconscious splitting, people with BP and
NP traits may truly believe that you are the most dangerous,
evil, immoral, crazy, or stupid person in the world. Therefore,
they may feel justified in treating you in one or more of these
extreme ways:

- Hitting you (domestic violence) or destroying your property

- Trying to keep you from leaving a room or the house

- Harassing you by phone or taking away your phone

- Hiding money

- Refusing to work

- Hurting the children

- Alienating the children

- Kidnapping the children

- Spreading rumors to your family and friends

- Using the court system to humiliate and control you

- Making false allegations of child abuse against you

- Making false allegations of domestic violence against you

- Making false allegations that *you* are alienating the children

- Making false allegations that you are hiding money

- Telling the court you can earn a lot of money but are
  unwilling

Therefore, to prepare for a separation and divorce, your immediate priority must be your physical safety and that of any children involved. You will also need to write down the details of behavior problems and confrontations right away so that you can respond to false statements your soon-to-be ex might make. This doesn't have to be overwhelming. It just takes organizing yourself in specific ways to deal with these fairly predictable problems. The more prepared you are for this pattern of extreme behavior and statements that comes from unconscious splitting, the better able you may be to keep your case from spinning out of control.

# An Assertive Approach

Regardless of where you are right now in the separation and divorce process, we recommend an assertive approach (in contrast to an aggressive or passive approach) in dealing with the potential splitting that may already have begun. We will explain this in more depth in chapter 4, but briefly, an assertive approach involves actively learning about personality problems, cultivating energy for dealing with such problems, documenting events (what happened and what was said), and actively presenting your information to legal professionals, the court, or both.

It's perfectly understandable and normal to feel like responding aggressively when someone acts aggressively toward you. You might try to eliminate your partner from your life and from your children's lives, or trash her the way she trashed you, but this common mistake backfires in court. Legal professionals may view you as the splitter and an equal party (or the primary party!) engaged in misbehavior. Even if that isn't true, you don't want to give your partner any ammunition to use against you in or out of court. An aggressive approach by you can increase your partner's unwanted behavior. Resist the urge to act aggressively, and mentally prepare yourself; in the long run you will be very glad you did.

A passive approach, the next most common mistake, is equally problematic. While it may be tempting to give up or give in on some or all of the issues in the divorce to avoid conflict, we don't recommend it. Just when you think you have given up enough that the partner with BP or NP traits should be satisfied, he may demand even more concessions. If you don't correct false statements about yourself, these statements may follow you into other parts of your life and possibly create future legal problems. You don't want to allow your partner to push you around, make false statements about you, and persuade others that you should be punished and restricted by the court.

If you're a classic avoider of conflict, changing the way you meekly respond to blame and criticism may be difficult—but change it you must. Court professionals don't have much time to make assessments, and first impressions really count. If you don't bring things up, it will be as if they never existed. Being passive didn't work during the marriage, and it doubly won't work now. The assertive approach doesn't have to be hard to understand and practice. An easy way to think about it is to focus on KEEP, an acronym that stands for *knowledge* and *energy* to *explain patterns*.

**Knowledge.** Informing yourself of the thinking and behavior patterns of people with BP and NP traits will give you a sense of relief (it's not about you!) and help you recognize and predict problems throughout your separation and divorce. That is the focus of the next chapter.

**Energy.** The problems of people with BP and NP traits can suck you dry. This is true when you live with them, and possibly even more so when you separate. It may take months, even years, to reach a reasonable outcome. Pace yourself and build your energy. This will be the focus of chapter 5.

**Explain.** The way you explain your partner's behavior to legal professionals is highly important. Using the assertive approach, you will focus on providing information rather than allowing your emotions to take over and cause you to become too aggres-sive or hold back too much. This will show a large contrast between you and a partner with BP or NP traits, who may present information in a highly emotional manner. This means that you will keep good records of important events and then present this information in detail to decision makers. This is the focus of much of part 2, "Succeeding in Family Court."

**Patterns.** From the start, think about how you will explain your partner's behavior patterns. Remember, legal professionals are still mostly unaware of personality disorders and their related issues. You can't just say, "Oh, she's a borderline, so you know what that means in terms of parenting," or "He's a narcissist, so you know why I need protection." Instead, you must present the details of these patterns, based on your record of events during your relationship and the separation process. (Remember, avoid labeling the person as having a personality disorder in court unless a formal diagnosis has already been accepted by the judge, which is rare. We will explain why in part 2.)

# Handling Issues Out of Court

An assertive approach also includes making strategic decisions about managing your case out of court and in the future. An easy way to remember this is to use another acronym: CALM, which stands for *consider alternatives* to *litigation* and *manage* your postdivorce relationship.

**Consider alternatives to litigation.** You don't have to go to court. The majority of divorces (and parenting decisions, when the partners are unmarried) are decided out of court by agreement of the parties. There are many factors to consider. Trying out-of-court alternatives may help your soon-to-be ex remain calmer and help you avoid encountering even more extreme behaviors. It's usually worthwhile to try methods like:

+ Mediation

+ Collaborative divorce

+ Negotiation through attorneys

+ A parenting coordinator

These methods, which we'll go into further in part 3, may save you significant time, money, and trauma. But these alternatives often don't work with people who have severe BP or NP traits, so you still need to be prepared to go to court. The assertive approach is about making rational choices, rather than overreacting (the aggressive approach) or just giving up (the passive approach).

**Manage your postdivorce relationship.** Many people are surprised and frustrated that a borderline or narcissistic ex may still be in their lives even after a divorce. You may be tempted to eliminate your ex from your life or, at the other extreme, become close again. Resist either urge. Each of these approaches will trigger more drama and trauma. As with everything else about the assertive approach, rationally consider all your alternatives and develop an arm's-length relationship that can give you stability in your future. We address how to do this in chapter 16.

In short, just remember the two acronyms: KEEP CALM. It's a simple way to remember to use an assertive approach without overreacting or giving up.

# There Is Hope

In preparing yourself for a separation or divorce, regardless of where you are in the process, keep in mind that thousands of people have managed the process well by using methods like those described in this book. It doesn't have to be complicated if you stick with the basic principles of an assertive approach. Remember, your divorce is a process that may last several months and sometimes years. You can make mistakes, learn from them, and correct them. Nobody's perfect, and given the nature of these difficult but charming personality types, few of their partners understand what they are getting into when they marry them.

You are not alone. Many others are going through similar situations. Knowledge and public discussion of the problems of people with BP and NP traits is growing. They are not bad people, and they want to be happy too. They didn't choose to have a personality disorder and don't understand how they sabotage themselves. They truly can't see the impact of their own behavior. We have a lot of empathy for them and want them to get the help they need—but this cannot be your responsibility.

# Conclusion

The biggest problem in a difficult divorce is usually a personality problem, especially when one of the partners has BP or NP traits. One of the key characteristics of such personalities is the unconscious dynamic of splitting people into all good and all bad, which can result in extreme behavior when the person experiences a profound loss of attachment, self-image, control, or some combination. Using an assertive approach can help you succeed in family court and out of court, which we describe in depth in the chapters ahead.

By separating and getting divorced, you are embarking on a new life. Pace yourself. We will help you navigate this process. You have already started to increase your knowledge. Now, let's take a look at BP and NP traits in more detail.

# Chapter 2

# Understanding Borderline and Narcissistic (and Antisocial) Personalities

*Sarah met Sam at a party. After an exciting two-month romance, they moved in together. Soon Sarah became pregnant, and they were married. Strangely, Sam started to view the pregnancy as a threat to his importance in Sarah's life, and he began occasionally hitting Sarah. He even punched her in the stomach when she was six months pregnant.*

*When Thomas met Tammy, he found her to be extremely outgoing, warm, and affectionate—but all this seemed to change after they got married. She became more and more moody, sometimes raging at him, and other times becoming depressed and withdrawn. Thomas wondered what could cause such a change in her personality.*

# Personality Disorders

People with personality disorders often seem to have two personalities. Their problems aren't obvious until you have known them for several months or see them in a crisis. They may appear normal or very exciting during courtship. They might be quite reasonable at work and with friends. But after you get really close to them for an extended period of time, they're no longer able to keep up this false self. They revert to their usual dysfunctional, extreme behavior. By then, it's usually too late to easily go separate ways.

Unfortunately, most people with personality disorders don't take responsibility for their actions. They think they're acting appropriately. They become surprised and angry when other people get upset with them. They have poor problem-solving skills and blame other people for "making them" act in extreme ways that twist their personal and professional lives into knots.

Personality disorders (PDs) usually begin in childhood or adolescence. While others around adults with PDs fervently wish they would change, it doesn't happen without a strong commitment and years of therapy. Most people with PDs are heavily in denial about their behavior. By the time they're adults, it's an automatic reaction for them to blame everything on the other person in a relationship.

Many people have some traits of a PD without actually having the disorder, but they can still create the conditions for a high-conflict divorce. Some people are hesitant to believe that a partner has a PD because the person hasn't been officially diagnosed. But getting a diagnosis is rare, because high-functioning people with PDs don't usually contact therapists—they don't think they need help. This book will help you, whether or not a clinician has made a firm diagnosis.

## A Hidden Problem

The *Diagnostic and Statistical Manual of Mental Disorders* is the "bible" used by mental health professionals to diagnose mental disorders. The fifth edition of this manual was published by the American Psychiatric Association in 2013 and is commonly referred to as the *DSM-5*. It lists ten personality disorders and their criteria (APA 2013). The two most common in high-conflict divorces appear to be BPD and NPD, and sometimes a person has both disorders or traits of both.

However, we are also seeing people with antisocial personality disorder (ASPD) involved in more and more high-conflict cases. It's not unusual that ASPD traits overlap with NPD and sometimes BPD, or that ASPD traits are confused with NPD traits. Each of these disorders has specific, predictable traits, which we will describe.

---

**Cautionary Note:** Only a well-trained professional can accurately make a diagnosis. Even professionals disagree, because these disorders are confusing and can remain hidden for a long time. Therefore, don't try to diagnose a PD yourself. BE SURE TO KEEP YOUR OPINION ABOUT A POSSIBLE DIAGNOSIS TO YOURSELF; DON'T SAY IT TO YOUR PARTNER, NO MATTER HOW TEMPTING IT MAY BE. This is the only sentence you will see in this whole book in all caps—that's how important this piece of advice is. It will backfire badly, triggering extreme anger and defensiveness. (As you will see later, it can also backfire to mention the diagnosis in court.)

---

## Borderline Personality Disorder

People with BPD typically feel unworthy and empty, lack a sense of self, and constantly fear real or imagined abandonment. They have some or all of these characteristics:

- Sudden and intense anger

- Wide, rapid mood swings

- Impulsive behavior, often regretted but sometimes defended as justified

- Substance abuse, eating disorders, or other potentially self-harming behavior

- Potentially violent actions, with a buildup of tension, an explosion of rage, and then remorse

- Impaired, black-and-white thinking, called "splitting." People with BPD put their partners on pedestals at the beginning of the relationship and then push them off when their partners are unable to meet all their demands. Splitting is a major contributor to high-conflict divorce.

- Great fear of abandonment, which nearly always comes into play during a divorce—even if *they* initiate the divorce. Ironically, the combination of intense clinging and intense anger tends to push people away.

People with BPD may also:

- Purposely or unconsciously selectively use sensitive information (such as finances, pregnancy, illness, or serious problems) to sway others to their viewpoint

- Seek revenge—for example, by destroying important personal possessions or spreading rumors

- Seek vindication—for example, by demanding loyalty and endless reassurance, and filing lawsuits

They usually deny responsibility for any of the previously noted behaviors.

*Thomas's wife, Tammy, has the characteristics of someone with BPD, although she has not been diagnosed. She has had a short fuse since she was a teenager, frequently becoming enraged at the people closest to her. Her parents learned to tolerate her and often gave in to her angry demands. They didn't argue with her when she erroneously blamed them for all her problems.*

*Thomas and Tammy have been married for five years and have a daughter, Brianna, aged four. Tammy blames Thomas when things go poorly for her, and she even yells and occasionally throws things at him. Once she threw a can of soup that hit him in the back of the head.*

*Thomas works full time, and even though Tammy works part time, she often expects him to take the primary role in caring for their daughter. Tammy finds Brianna irritating and has little patience for the messes she makes. Patient and tolerant, Thomas often gets up in the middle of the night and helps Brianna, especially when Tammy is in one of her bad moods.*

*Thomas is considering divorcing Tammy, but he's worried. In the chapters ahead, Tammy will demonstrate many common behaviors of someone with BPD who is facing a divorce, while Thomas will deal with many predictable dilemmas.*

## Narcissistic Personality Disorder

People with this specific PD often have some or all of these characteristics:

- Are self-absorbed and indifferent to the needs of others

- Believe they are superior to others

- Are very charming, exciting, and persuasive

- Lack empathy for others (although they may mouth the customary words)

- Are highly sensitive to criticism or perceived insults

- Fear being seen as inferior or helpless

- Have a sense of entitlement, or the feeling that they're owed special treatment for no apparent reason

- Are demanding of attention and admiration

- Are demeaning and insulting to people closest to them, sometimes in public

- Regularly complain about being a victim and being taken advantage of

They usually deny responsibility for any of the preceding behaviors.

As with BPD, many of these behaviors were ordinary human traits that became extreme, long-standing, and pervasive. Being self-centered can be healthy in small doses; it helps us get through minor criticisms and setbacks. It becomes a symptom of a PD when the characteristics repeatedly and negatively affect the person's personal and social lives.

People with NPD often inspire anger in the people around them. Their self-sabotaging behavior invites insult and criticism rather than the respect they desperately want. A *narcissistic injury* occurs when the narcissist encounters a threat (real or imagined) to the narcissist's belief that he is perfect and entitled to special treatment and recognition. Narcissists crave admiration and attention from others. Criticism, disagreement, and a perceived slight or insult can lead to *narcissistic rage*, a reaction disproportional to the "offense."

Sarah's husband, Sam, has the characteristics of NPD, although he has never sought counseling and never been diagnosed. Self-centered and believing himself to be superior, he can be very charming and likes to show off. But when he is stressed or feels like a failure, he can be very verbally abusive and sometimes physically abusive. He demands respect and admiration, even when there's no reason why he would deserve it.

After baby Jay was born, Sam became increasingly disdainful and demeaning toward Sarah: "You're ugly and fat now. Who would want you?" Sam got angry when Sarah's cousin, who lived nearby, helped out with the baby: "I can take care of anything you need. Are you saying I'm not providing for you? You're my wife, and I come first!"

It was easier for Sarah to just give in rather than stick up for herself. Slowly, she felt increasingly isolated, cut off from her friends and family. Sam seemed to want complete control over her and the baby. Sam referred to Jay as "my" son, not "our" son. He saw a bright future for Jay and continued to put Sarah down. The physical abuse didn't go away: he shoved and hit her, occasionally leaving bruises. Sometimes he apologized but not always. Sarah had been physically abused as a child and was used to accepting this type of behavior. If anyone asked about her bruises, she would just make up a story about being clumsy.

Sarah doesn't know what to do. She wants to protect their son and wants the violence to stop, but she's afraid of upsetting Sam. She believes that they truly love each other, and she doesn't want to leave him. But the relationship is clearly not working. We'll see what happens when she separates from him and they go to court.

## Antisocial Personality Disorder

People with this PD often have some or all of these characteristics:

- Are chronic liars, even when they can be easily caught

- Are con artists, sometimes faking an identity and living a secret separate life

- Are highly aggressive, risk taking, fast talking, and sometimes very impulsive

- Like to dominate others, sometimes using violence to get what they want inside and outside the family

- May enjoy humiliating and hurting others, destroying their property, reputations, and lives

- Lack remorse and will do whatever it takes to get what they want, including breaking the law

- May be con artists in business, fabricating records, avoiding taxes, borrowing heavily or stealing outright—often without the knowledge of their family

- Can be very charming, constantly advertising their "good deeds," looking and sounding sincere

- Can be skilled at claiming they are victims to get empathy, avoid consequences, and shift blame to others

- Enjoy manipulating family members, friends, counselors, lawyers, judges, mediators, and others

You may note some similarities between narcissists and antisocials, yet the *DSM-5* says that narcissists do not have the qualities of deception, aggression, and impulsivity that antisocials have (APA 2013, 662). If you see those characteristics, you are more likely to be observing an ASPD. However, some people have traits of both NPD and ASPD. In divorce cases, what stands out about those with ASPD is the constant lying and fabrication of events, plus the willingness to hurt their spouses and/or families without remorse. Narcissists exaggerate, want to look good, care about what you think of them, and don't usually intend to hurt you. On the other hand, antisocials really don't care and often enjoy other people's pain.

Overall, from our observations, there appear to be fewer antisocial personalities involved in protracted family court cases than narcissistic and borderline personalities, because they are impatient and don't like to feel dominated by the court or the court procedures. However, when ASPDs feel successful at fooling professionals and the courts, they can dig in and create some of the worst court cases that we have seen.

Here are some antisocial examples:

*Penny separated from her husband of six years. In the divorce process, she discovered that he never held a job during their marriage even though he pretended to go to work each day. Instead, he was skimming money out of her father's business. In addition, he was spending money on prostitutes and internet sex calls. Penny never had a clue that any of this was going on, which isn't surprising because people with ASPD can con everyone.*

Another example:

*Stephanie ended up in several years of court battles over custody of her two children with her ex-husband. He repeatedly made claims to the court that she was blocking him from a reasonable relationship with the children. He said she was giving them too much medication, preventing them from participating in the soccer team he coached, getting them late to school, driving them without seat belts fastened, and on and on. At first, his concerns grabbed the attention of the judge, who sharply criticized Stephanie for her inappropriate behavior at one hearing after another. This would have been understandable if any of his allegations were true. But they weren't. It took Stephanie over two years of providing detailed evidence before the judge started to understand that her ex-husband was lying about everything and had manipulated the court into feeling sorry for him.*

Yet another example:

*Larry's wife was physically abusive with him, which really embarrassed him and he didn't tell anyone at first. She controlled their finances and he was certain she was hiding money in unknown accounts. He once obtained a restraining order against her after she pushed him over backwards in his chair, causing a cut on his head. But then he decided not to have the restraining order papers served on her and never told her about it while they continued to live together.*

*Then she took up with a boyfriend who was very aggressive and lied about everything. Larry found them together once and the boyfriend punched him in the face. Then they conspired to say Larry assaulted the boyfriend and injured his arm. They pursued a criminal trial against Larry. The divorce proceeded while the criminal trial was pending, a situation that his wife used to repeatedly prejudice the family court judge against Larry. After all, he was accused of a felony assault by the district attorney. She appeared to enjoy lying and humiliating him in public. She found a family lawyer who enabled her in everything she wanted.*

*She successfully turned their three children against Larry, limiting his contact. At the criminal trial, a jury believed his now ex-wife and her boyfriend over what Larry said, as there were no other witnesses and they were emotionally persuasive blamers. But there were several irregularities in the case, and it was eventually thrown out on appeal. After more hearings on various absurd issues over the years, the ex-wife finally stopped taking Larry to court after the children were all adults. In the end, Larry was never found to have done anything wrong. But the financial, emotional, and career disruptions were devastating.*

## A Serious and Growing Problem

The *DSM-5* estimates that 15 percent of adults in the U.S. have a personality disorder (APA 2013, 646). Among professionals, these three are known as the most difficult and the most likely to show up in interpersonal disputes. They are all in the Cluster B grouping of personality disorders (along with histrionic personality disorder), which the *DSM-5* indicates tend to exhibit dramatic, emotional, or erratic behavior (APA 2013, 646).

According to the largest study ever conducted on PDs by the U.S. National Institutes of Health (NIH), 5.9 percent of the U.S. population have a BPD (Grant et al. 2008); 6.2 percent have NPD (Stinson et al. 2008); and 3.6 percent have ASPD (Grant et al. 2004). Because some people have two or three of these overlapping disorders, this means that about 10 percent of adults in the U.S. have BPD, NPD, and/or ASPD. Yet these statistics have probably increased over the last two decades, as we have observed and many mental health and legal professionals have also reported.

This study looked at PDs by age group and found that each younger age group has a higher incidence of these disorders. This means that about 10 percent of people aged thirty to forty-four and over 15 percent of people aged twenty to twenty-nine meet the criteria for one or more of these three disorders (Grant et al. 2008; Stinson et al. 2008). Since personality doesn't change much throughout a lifetime, these disorders appear to us to be increasing with each younger generation, although the research did not reach any conclusion about why this may be.

Of the people meeting the criteria for a BPD diagnosis, 53 percent were women and 47 percent were men (Grant et al. 2008), and of the people meeting the criteria for NPD, 62 percent were men and 38 percent were women (Stinson et al. 2008). But college students' scores on the Narcissistic Personality Inventory indicate that young women are increasingly narcissistic and closing the gap with men (Twenge and Campbell 2009), so these gender percentages are not significant enough to make any assumptions about men or women predominantly having one or the other disorder. Your partner could have either disorder—or both. Almost 40 percent of people with one of these disorders also have the other, according to the NIH study (Grant et al. 2008; Stinson et al. 2008).

ASPD is much more heavily male at 74 percent, while women are only 26 percent (Grant et al. 2004). Yet antisocial women can be very harmful, as Larry's case example shows above. It appears that ASPD is a more genetically based disorder, such that first-degree biological relatives (such as children) are more likely to inherit this than in the general population (APA 2013, 661). This is a tendency and not a certainty, as life events may increase or decrease this risk.

In addition to these statistics, it's important to know that many more people have *some traits* of a PD, but not the full disorder. Therefore, the number of people with some of these problems may be even higher. Reports we get when we speak to people in other countries, including Canada, European countries, Australia, and Japan, confirm that these personality problems are similar in many modern societies. We are facing a worldwide relationship problem that few people even know exists.

# Risk Factors for Borderline Personality Disorder

. PET scans and MRI techniques have made it possible to see how the brains of people with BPD function differently from other people's brains. A part of the brain called the *amygdala*, which lies in the limbic system, controls the intensity of our emotions and our ability to return to normal after sharp emotions have been aroused. Brain scans show that in people with BPD, the amygdala is more active than in control subjects. Malfunctions in neurotransmitter levels, as well as other abnormalities in the neurotransmitter system, can lead to problems such as impaired reasoning, impulsivity, and unstable emotions (Friedel 2004).

Parents who have one child with BPD and another one without the disorder may wonder why the two children are different. The answer may be in our genes. There appear to be at least two, and perhaps four or five, genes that influence the traits that make up BPD. Different genes may control problems with impulsivity, emotional regulation, or the thinking and perceiving powers of the brain. It isn't BPD that can be inherited; instead, it's the traits that, taken together, make up BPD that are passed on: traits like aggressiveness, depression, excitability, quickness to anger, and susceptibility to addiction (Friedel 2006).

Following are childhood experiences within the family that can increase the likelihood that someone who is biologically predisposed to BPD will develop the disorder (Friedel 2004; Friedel 2006):

* Emotional, sexual, or physical abuse, though not everyone who has been abused has BPD, and not everyone who has BPD has been abused

• Ineffective parenting or perceived ineffective parenting

• A poor match between the temperaments and personalities of parent and child

• Home situations that intensify the negative perceptions of the child

• Sudden loss or perceived abandonment, which can arise from something like a divorce or even displacement by a new baby

## Treatment for BPD

The great news is that new forms of treatment for BPD are showing success, although it's impossible to force someone to seek treatment. Threats and ultimatums (such as "Go to therapy, or I will leave you") don't work for long, because therapy is hard work. For those who are willing to seek therapy, medication is one important approach. While there's no pill for BPD, medications can help reduce its symptoms, such as depression, mood swings, dissociation, aggression, and impulsivity. Medication classes used include antipsychotics, antidepressants, and mood stabilizers (Friedel 2004).

Several structured programs exist that target people with BPD who are motivated to work on their problems. These structured treatments seem to produce better results than treatment as usual (Farrell, Shaw, and Webber 2009; Fonagy and Luyten 2009) and include:

• Dialectical behavior therapy (DBT) (Linehan 1993)

• Mentalization based therapy (MBT) (Fonagy and Luyten 2009)

• Schema therapy (Farrell, Shaw, and Webber 2009)

• STEPPS group treatment

All of these treatments include several factors that may help them achieve success:

- Specialized clinician training, which gives them more effective tools

- Clinician education, which gives treatment providers a more positive attitude about recovery and working with patients

- Treatment twice a week instead of once a week

- The opportunity to interact with peers who have the same disorder

Unfortunately, these structured treatments are not widely available. The person with BPD who is seeking a local clinician should focus on these characteristics:

- The clinician's experience and education are specific to BPD.

- The clinician believes that recovery is possible.

- The clinician knows about the latest research and understands the role of brain disorder in people with BPD.

- The clinician can articulate specific goals for therapy that are realistic, especially within the time limits that a health insurance plan might set for the therapy.

- The clinician has support from colleagues for treating BPD.

- The clinician is confident in her own ability and savvy about how people with BPD can behave. The professional is compassionate toward the person with BPD, but smart enough not to get sucked in emotionally by the person's dysfunctional ways of relating to others, especially to therapists.

## Risk Factors for Narcissistic Personality Disorder

In contrast to BPD, genetic or brain differences don't seem to play a role in the development of NPD. Instead, the risk factors focus on social learning (Millon 1996). The first is the issue of an "insecure attachment" in the parent-child relationship in very early childhood. Child development researchers have discovered that some infants avoid their parents' reassurance when they are upset, even as early as twelve months old (Wallin 2007). They are considered to have an *avoidant* or *dismissive* attachment, which can have serious implications because a secure attachment in early childhood is the foundation for all future relationships on into adulthood. Avoidant attachment has been identified as a risk factor for NPD (ibid.).

Without a secure early childhood attachment, a child may not:

◆ Learn to reflect on himself and his own feelings

◆ Develop a secure sense of herself in the world

◆ Learn empathy

◆ Believe in secure future relationships

◆ Learn to modulate his narcissistic distress and rage

This insecure attachment style is thought to be the result of a poor fit between parent and child, perhaps because of the child's difficult temperament at birth, the parent's poor parenting skills, or both. This attachment style can also be the result of child abuse, from which the child learns to distrust others (Schore 2003).

Thus the child copes by growing up aloof, having a sense of superiority (*I don't need anyone; I'm special*), and a hypersensitivity to criticism and disrespect. Throughout childhood, the narcissist may repeatedly respond to minor events with disdainful comments and extreme narcissistic rage. Because this coping method is learned in infancy, the person has no awareness of this sense of vulnerability and instead develops an inflated self-image, which she really believes! Some studies of narcissists show that they consciously and *unconsciously* have higher self-esteem than others (Twenge and Campbell 2009). But they repeatedly experience narcissistic injuries when they are criticized or have even the smallest weakness exposed.

The second major risk factor for NPD appears to be the absorption of cultural changes in our modern society in personality development. In their book *The Narcissism Epidemic: Living in the Age of Entitlement*, Jean Twenge and Keith Campbell (2009) describe a significant preoccupation with individualism and self-esteem beginning in the 1970s in the United States and around the world. Since then, parents, teachers, and others have promoted the idea (theoretically good) that children should grow up loving themselves and believing that they are special and that they can do and be anything. Unfortunately, in reality, these ideas have been taken to an extreme and separated from making an effort and learning necessary skills. People instead simply feel entitled to the rewards of life without working for them, and they become angry or depressed when these rewards don't come pouring in.

In particular, parenting styles have changed significantly over the past fifty years, so that children grow up with a sense of entitlement because parents have been taught to overvalue and indulge them. Rather than learn to get along with others, the child learns to be self-centered and to put her own needs above those of the rest of the family, including the parents. The children of such parenting are protected from the negative consequences of their own behavior, so that they don't learn the give-and-take of adult social relationships and don't learn how to control their own behavior—symptoms of NPD (Millon 1996).

While most people raised over the past fifty years have not developed NPD, the numbers are dramatically increasing. The large NIH study released in 2008 (Stinson et al. 2008) stated that 6.2 percent of the general U.S. population have NPD, whereas the *DSM* research reported in 1994 stated that NPD was diagnosed in less than 1 percent of the general population (APA 1994, 660). Of course, this may be partially the result of different research methods and the size of the more recent study.

## Treatment for NPD

There's no great news about treatment for NPD, because most people with this disorder avoid getting help unless under duress from family members or employers. Successful methods have focused on cognitive behavioral skills (step-by-step changes in thinking and behavior) in the context of a supportive, but challenging, therapy relationship. There's no pill specifically for NPD, but medications may help reduce the impact of other problems the person with NPD often experiences, such as depression, anxiety, and bipolar disorder.

The most important factor in treatment for NPD is the therapist. Most therapists are not trained to balance supportive methods and challenging methods in their work with narcissists. They are either too supportive (which reinforces the narcissist's bad behavior or makes it worse) or too confrontational (which narcissists really can't handle, so they quit therapy). Cognitive behavioral therapy programs, such as schema therapy, have had some success with narcissists (Young, Klosko, and Weishaar 2003). People with NPD also seem to benefit from alcohol and drug treatment programs, because the skills for recovery (looking at their own part in problems rather than thinking they themselves are so special) help them rein in their narcissism without feeling singled out for criticism or blame.

# Risk Factors for Antisocial Personality Disorder

Some of the parties involved in high-conflict divorces have antisocial personality disorder or its traits, and there are many who have ASPD combined with BPD or NPD. According to the NIH study, about 19 percent of people with ASPD also have BPD (Grant et al. 2008), and about 21 percent of people with ASPD also have NPD (Stinson et al. 2008).

People with ASPD have some biological differences from other people. Even when they are adopted at a very early age, they have more in common with their biological parents than their adoptive ones (APA 2013). This suggests that the strongest factor for many of those with this personality disorder is genetic—that they are born this way.

But there are also people who have ASPD as a result of terrible abuse in childhood, so that they cannot connect in normal relationships with others. It's not surprising to have a creepy feeling around them, triggering concerns for your own safety. On the other hand, they can be such con artists that they persuade you to trust them while they steal from you or harm you in some other way. The general principles of protecting yourself in this book also apply to an antisocial partner.

## Treatment for ASPD

We know of no truly effective treatment for people with ASPD once they become adults. Their antisocial behavior appears to be hardwired into their personalities. There has been some treatment success at reducing antisocial behavior and strengthening relationship skills in adolescents with ASPD. As adults, they actually get worse in individual therapy, because they con the therapist and learn psychological skills to be even more manipulative. They often sabotage group therapies, such as treatment groups for batterers, because they are not motivated and enjoy dominating and manipulating professionals.

While we don't emphasize people with ASPD in this book, we will point out areas where they pose slightly different problems from people with BPD and NPD. In general, people with ASPD demonstrate many of the same problems, but sometimes spend less time fighting in a divorce, because there are too many people involved for them to manipulate and they don't like being dominated by the court. They don't really care about the children, so they may not fight over them much, in contrast to borderlines and narcissists, who are often preoccupied with the children.

Many people with ASPD have a criminal record and lie so much that their behavior patterns are more obvious to the court. They often are involved in shady financial schemes and avoid their financial responsibilities to the family. Even when they lose in court on financial matters, their antisocial behavior helps them avoid ever paying what they owe. They often just take the money and run.

# Think of Patterns, Not Disorders

Don't try to figure out whether your partner has an actual PD or mere traits. Even mental health professionals often disagree about this, and their "bible" of diagnosis, the *DSM*, changes every few years. It doesn't really matter, because the strategies we give you will work whether or not the person has traits or an actual disorder, and there's no need to "prove" a diagnosis in court. Instead, if necessary, you will describe the *patterns* of your partner's behavior in your own situation, as we explain in later chapters.

# Conclusion

BPD, NPD, and ASPD patterns of behavior can include rapid mood swings, sudden anger, impulsive behavior, potential violence, and a great fear of being abandoned, losing an inflated self-image, or losing control over others (you). The person can be extremely charming, exciting, and persuasive, but also exceedingly self-absorbed, arrogant, disdainful, aggressive, deceitful, and lacking in empathy and remorse. In a difficult divorce, these personality characteristics can play a much larger role than the legal issues, but they can affect the legal process at every step.

In the next chapter, we will explain how these personality patterns often escalate in a divorce and then how you can use your knowledge to manage them. As we close this chapter, we will remind you once again: don't tell your partner you think he or she has a personality disorder. This will trigger defensiveness and possible retaliation that will make your case much more difficult, perhaps for years to come.

Chapter 3

# Blamers and Targets:
# It's All Your Fault!

After enough incidents of being shoved, hit, and kicked by Sam, Sarah, with the help of her cousin, got up the nerve to go to court and ask for a restraining order. She didn't really want a divorce; she only wanted Sam to change. She got a restraining order based on her description of only one incident. She held back the full history of abuse, because she did not want to upset Sam too much. But after she got the temporary restraining order (TRO) papers, she changed her mind and never had them served on Sam, so they expired.

Finally, after more abuse, she again went to court, got a new TRO, and had the papers served on Sam; he was ordered to move out of the house and stay at least a hundred yards away from her. At their first full hearing, Sarah was surprised to see that Sam had an attorney (she had none).

Sam's attorney argued persuasively that the allegations against Sam were false and that he should get custody of their son, Jay, now one year old. He alleged that Sarah was a depressed pill addict who hit the child, gave him tranquilizers to keep him quiet, and left him unattended to wander in the house while she slept all day.

Sam provided two declarations (signed statements filed with the court), one from a friend and one from his sister, who said Sarah had told her that the bruises were from being clumsy (which Sarah actually told her once). Both declarations swore that Sam had never been violent with anyone, that he was a very caring father, and that Sarah was mentally unstable.

None of this was true, but Sarah was in shock. She knew she had seen her doctor for sleeping pills and overslept on one occasion. But at court, she felt guilty and was unable to speak up in her own defense against Sam's aggressive attorney and his declarations. She had merely tried to protect herself and was now a target of blame—unprepared to defend herself and unable to explain the full story of Sam's abusive behavior toward her.

After five years of marriage, Thomas decided he could no longer tolerate Tammy's mood swings and frequent rages. When Thomas told Tammy he wanted a divorce, she threw an iron at him and smashed a window in his car. "How can you leave me after all I've done for you?" she screamed. "You'll be sorry!"

Thomas suggested that they handle their whole divorce with an out-of-court mediator, but Tammy refused to do anything to help make the divorce happen. So, Thomas filed for a court hearing, asking for equally shared custody of Brianna and reasonable child and spousal support for Tammy.

Before their hearing, they were required to attend a mediation session with a family court counselor to try to resolve any parenting issues. During the mediation session, Tammy informed the court counselor that Thomas had sexually *abused Brianna and that he should therefore only have very limited, supervised visits with the child. Thomas strongly denied any abuse, but Tammy could be a very persuasive blamer when she was upset.*

# Increased Splitting

Sarah and Thomas were not prepared for the predictable behavior patterns of people with BP, NP, or ASP traits in a separation and divorce. As we first mentioned in chapter 1, "splitting" is the mental health term used to describe the unconscious coping mechanism of seeing situations and people in extremes of all good and all bad. Sometimes, people with BP traits see themselves as all bad, and they may become depressed or suicidal. At other times, they may see themselves as all good and see you—the divorcing partner—as all bad. This can have a domino effect, because they also often view legal and psychiatric professionals as all good or all bad, which engenders a lot of conflict.

## Key Times of Risk of Extreme Behavior

Splitting increases whenever someone with BPD, NPD, or ASPD *senses* a relationship loss. For people with BP traits, this loss usually has to do with fear of abandonment. People with NP traits fear being inferior, the loss of their inflated self-image. Those with ASP traits fear loss of dominance, the ability to have someone around who must obey them. All fear loss of control, because they feel so out of control emotionally. Therefore, you can predict that your partner's view of you, and behavior toward you, will suddenly become more extreme at key times of risk, including the following:

- You say you want to separate.

- You separate.

- You make requests (no matter how reasonable) that represent loss to your partner.

- You serve papers on your partner that request court orders he or she won't like.

- You attend a court hearing to get orders your partner won't like.

- The court makes orders against your partner.

- Your partner loses more time with the child than he or she expected.

- Your partner has less contact with you than he or she expected.

- Your legal case ends.

- You start a new relationship, get married, or have a child.

- Your former partner experiences a major setback in his own life later on.

- You or your partner seek to modify custody, support, or both later on.

You may view each of these events with a sense of hope and relief. Finally, you are bringing an end to the chaos, fear, and emotional and financial drain on your life! But the opposite may be true. Freedom for you may be an intolerable loss for your partner, or so it may feel to them.

First, you must protect yourself from physical danger and prepare for the court process (even while making efforts to resolve your case out of court).

## Physical Safety

Today's news features more and more stories about people who are undergoing a divorce seriously harming a partner, the children, or both. While such events are still rare, they are a warning to consider physical danger at the key times just described. Since people with BP, NP, or ASP traits have predictable patterns of behavior, think about your partner's past behavior.

- Has your partner made threats of violence toward you or your children?

- Does your partner have a history of violent or impulsive behavior?

- Does your partner have a substance-abuse problem?

- Does your partner have easy access to weapons?

All of these items are potential risks for physical harm when you're involved with someone with BPD, NPD, or ASPD, and all must be taken seriously.

In most murder cases, there were warning signs of serious danger—but not always. Sometimes you will have a gut feeling that tells you physical protection may be necessary. In many cases, leading up to the murder there was a series of recent losses, such as:

- A job loss

- Loss of a house

- Separation from a partner

- Significantly reduced contact with a child

- A change of custody

- The loss of a pet or other property

Some people with BPD, NPD, or ASPD can't handle this growing series of losses when they sense no hope for their future. With domestic violence perpetrators (who, in Bill's observation, are mostly people with BPD, NPD, or ASPD), the risk of violence can be highest at the time of separation, because the partner with the PD tries to stop the losses of attachment, inflated self-image, dominance, and control.

Repeated losses in court may add up to an increased risk of danger later in the case. Many cases in the news refer to the violent actions of a distraught partner who expects to lose contact with, or custody of, a child at an upcoming hearing. In some cases, the risk is highest when the battle finally ends and the fantasies of continued contact with and control of you through the court process are over.

If you're concerned about your physical safety, find out about resources in your area, including domestic violence hotlines, and consult a therapist or lawyer as soon as possible to evaluate your risk. Ideally, you should do this before even discussing a separation or divorce with your partner. But consider physical safety *throughout your case*, especially at each of the key times previously described.

## The Court Process of Splitting

The adversarial court process encourages conflict and worsens unconscious splitting in a partner with a PD. The court environment is based on pitting two people against each other, splitting people into extremes of all good and all bad: plaintiff versus defendant, injured party versus guilty party, victim versus perpetrator.

This legal reinforcement of splitting can be extremely threatening to the fragile identity and deep insecurities of someone with BP, NP, or ASP traits. It can encourage that partner's exaggerations and fears when legal professionals take her seriously and courts provide him or her with a forum for putting all of the blame on the other person, the "bad partner." The result is a potentially high-conflict dispute that can surprise everyone, including the family of the partner with the PD and the professionals involved.

# Persuasive Blamers and Their Targets

Not all people with BP, NP, or ASP traits become embroiled in high-conflict divorce disputes. Those who do are a subgroup we call "persuasive blamers" or simply "blamers." The following chart indicates the characteristics of the subgroup of people with BP, NP, or ASP traits who become persuasive blamers. People who drive high-conflict divorces in family courts exhibit the same characteristics.

## Borderline and Narcissistic Blamers

|  | Borderline | Narcissistic |
|---|---|---|
| *General characteristics:* | Fear of abandonment<br>Unstable sense of self<br>Unstable relationships<br>Impulsive<br>Frequent mood swings<br>Frequent anger<br>Easily feels abandoned | Fear of being inferior<br>Exaggerated sense of self<br>Self-absorbed<br>Wants excessive attention<br>Expects special treatment<br>Takes advantage of others<br>Lacks empathy |

|  | Borderline | Narcissistic |
|---|---|---|
| *Overcompensates with:* | Clinging behaviors | Constant bragging |
|  | Self-destructive acts | Disdain for others |
|  | Sudden and intense rage | Attacks if feels insulted |
|  | Efforts to control others to avoid feeling abandoned | Efforts to control others to avoid feeling inferior |
|  | Possible manipulation of others | Possible manipulation of others |
|  | Possible use of seductive charm | Possible use of seductive charm |
|  | Impulsive risk taking | Unawareness of own risk taking |
| *Additional characteristics of blamers subgroup:* | Blames a specific target (such as a partner, child, or professional) for feeling abandoned or inferior | |
|  | Repeatedly attacks or blames target with violence, verbal abuse, financial abuse, legal abuse, and so on; sees target as all bad (splitting) | |
|  | Has extreme emotional intensity about blaming target | |
|  | Launches personal attacks on target's intelligence and sanity | |
|  | Preoccupied with analyzing target's character traits | |
|  | Recruits others to attack target | |
|  | Seeks other professionals to blame target | |
|  | Seeks validation for own thinking and behavior | |
|  | Seeks retaliation against target | |
|  | Often sees court as most accessible source of power and control in our society | |

Persuasive blamers focus the blame for their problems on one specific person: a target of blame (or just "target"). Targets of blame are usually:

* Intimate partners

* People perceived to have authority, such as doctors, lawyers, clergy, police officers, managers, and government employees

In divorce, the target is most commonly the divorcing partner. But sometimes it becomes one of the children, the other partner's lawyer, the other partner's new romantic interest, or even the judge or mediator. As described next, blamers' cognitive distortions can be extreme and lead to extreme behavior.

## Cognitive Distortions

Cognitive distortions are automatic negative thoughts that don't fit the present reality. They just pop into our minds, usually from past experiences. Mental health professionals have identified several cognitive distortions, including the following (with an example of each in italics):

* All-or-nothing thinking: *You're perfect one day, an evil monster the next.*

* Jumping to conclusions: *Since you're evil, you must have done evil acts.*

* Emotional reasoning: *If the situation feels hopeless, then it must be hopeless.*

* Exaggerated fears: *I know you're out to get me.*

* Projection: *I see my own faults in others, but not at all in myself.*

Most people reflect on their own thoughts: *Is this true? Am I overreacting? I should check this out.* But people with PDs don't reflect on their own thoughts or behavior. Like someone who is drunk, their thinking is continually "under the influence" of their cognitive distortions. They can send, but not receive, new information. Because they are unaware of their cognitive distortions, these distortions can underlie serious misbehavior, including physical abuse, emotional abuse, and even legal abuse (using the legal system to attack a target and to promote false or unnecessary litigation).

Information that does not fit the distortion is rigidly, unconsciously blocked as too threatening and confusing. Instead, people with PDs defend their distortions in an effort to protect themselves. Blamers repeatedly react to "false alarms" caused by all-or-nothing thinking, jumping to conclusions, and so forth. They *truly believe* that they are in danger, and they feel powerless and out of control inside.

## Power and Control

To feel some sense of power and control, people with BPD, NPD, or ASPD strike out at those they perceive are hurting them—with physical violence, verbal abuse, hurtful rumors spread to family and friends (often called "distortion campaigns"), other actions, or some combination. All of these actions may *seem* necessary to their survival at the moment, although the disordered person may later regret them.

When a divorce is initiated, regardless of who files with the court, blamers particularly feel threatened. Many cannot handle seeming in any way responsible for the divorce, which triggers their lifelong fears of abandonment and inferiority. Therefore, they split their partner into all bad. It *feels* like a war between good and evil to blamers, so they create one. Their extreme feelings create their own problems.

# How Blamers Typically Behave in Family Court Cases

When borderline and narcissistic blamers enter the court system, you can anticipate a common, and sometimes severe, pattern of problems. The examples of Sarah and Thomas show some common behaviors encountered when blamers go to court.

## Blamers Aggressively Blame a Target

Blamers constantly misperceive events, and they experience overwhelming emotional distress and frequent interpersonal conflict. They view all problems as caused by external forces and truly don't understand why "bad things" happen to them. They chronically feel like helpless victims—even if they initiated the divorce—and are unable to reflect on or change their behavior. While the source of their problems may seem obvious to everyone else, they don't see it themselves (Beck et al. 1990). The number-one external focus of blame and focus of attack is the person closest to the blamer: *you*. When targets fight back, blamers intensify their attacks—with physical abuse, verbal abuse, distortion campaigns, or legal abuse—in frantic efforts to get others to change or to get revenge for perceived abandonment or narcissistic injuries. They think this will make them feel better.

Blamers pressure other people to take a position in this blaming war: "Either you're with me, or you're against me." The intensity of their anger and blame catches people off guard. Often, just to calm the person down, others will reluctantly join in the blaming of the target. This encourages the blamer to further pursue his or her distortion campaign, because cognitive distortions can be like a computer "virus," giving the blamer self-destructive information that looks like normal information.

When other people take the blamer's distortions at face value, it's like passing along a virus.

While BP, NP, and ASP blamers seek targets, their issues can be slightly different, as explained next, but some have all of the following dynamics. Recognize and anticipate these problems.

### Borderline Abandonment Rage

Mental health professionals are very familiar with the fear of abandonment of the person with BP traits. This fear may have served a very real purpose in childhood when the child's life depended on a secure bond with a parent. In adulthood, however, this fear often drives people away and is no longer productive. Regardless, people with BP traits alternate between the extremes of clinging behavior and rage when they feel their relationship security is in any way threatened. Once a divorce is obvious and clinging won't work (and again, it doesn't matter who initiated the divorce), they often become enraged against the perceived target. They may do anything to harm the target, both for revenge and for validation that they are innocent of any responsibility for the breakup.

They may physically batter their former loved one (Dutton 2007). They may attempt to dominate or alienate the children. They may make allegations that will publicly humiliate their partner. Sometimes they are conscious of the wrong they are doing, but it seems justified because of the intensity of their sense of abandonment. Sometimes they completely believe that their domestic violence is necessary: "She deserved it after what she did to me." And sometimes they truly believe in their false allegations of abuse, despite all the evidence to the contrary: "He must have harmed our child; I just know it, after what he did to me by abandoning me."

## Narcissistic Injury

Since divorce is seen as a failure, narcissists cannot tolerate any suggestion that they had a role in ending the marriage. After all, the narcissist is a "superior" person. It would be too much of a narcissistic injury to have any deficiencies as a partner, even though these flaws may have been a primary cause of the divorce. The divorce must be totally blamed on a person who is so "inferior" that it's all that person's fault.

Thus, while narcissists sometimes physically abuse their partners, they often will focus on making allegations of sexual or parenting defects against their partner—their target of blame. They may attempt to take over the role of the "only good parent" in a custody battle or visitation dispute. They may take or hide money, based on the belief that they deserve a larger share of the family resources, because they always feel entitled to "more." Since they feel so out of control, they attempt to control others to help themselves feel better, so they require a target on whom to focus all of their frustration and blame. This never solves any problems in the long run, because the problem is internal and must be worked on internally.

In daily life, most people quickly recognize that the target is not responsible for the blamer's problems. But in court, all allegations are taken seriously, and daily life is not observed; convincing the court is a process of persuasion, and blamers can be very persuasive.

## Antisocial Charm and Deceit

It's often very simple for those with ASP traits: they make up the whole thing. They often make false allegations of child abuse, domestic violence, alienation, substance abuse, and so forth, with no basis in reality at all. However, because they can be the most persuasive of all, their partners may be criticized and intensely blamed by the judge, lawyers, counselors, and others for various nonexistent or minor negative behaviors.

### Predictable Allegations

Blamers will try to persuade friends and family to falsely say in court that you are one or more of the following:

- A child abuser or molester

- A batterer

- A child alienator

- An alcoholic or addict

- A liar who makes false allegations

- A deadbeat dad who doesn't pay support

- An unfit mother who endangers the child

- Any other type of person who is all bad in our society

These allegations against you may even be influenced by recent news. In one case, a blamer falsely accused a father of child sexual abuse, domestic violence, and drug addiction. But then came the big shocker: she tried to persuade the court that he was a terrorist who knew about the September 11, 2001, World Trade Center attacks before they happened and failed to alert the authorities! These allegations were absurd, but he had to respond to each of them. Do prepare for this extreme splitting from the start and at each significant step along the way, as we will describe.

## Blamers Are Emotionally Persuasive

As we said, people with BPD, NPD, or ASPD who are persuasive blamers can be skilled at convincing others that it's all your fault. When they go to court, they often win at first, because they are so emotionally persuasive. Partners are often totally surprised to discover that they have become targets of blame in a formal, public setting, aggressively attacked by their former loved one: "I never imagined she would say or do these things in court." They are also surprised by the court's seemingly favorable responses: "How could the judge believe all of his false statements?" or "They're letting her get away with everything."

Since emotions add credibility and power to a person's statements, blamers are often believed early in the case. Others assume the target must have done *something* to have caused the blamer's distress, and thus they become convinced that the blamer is really a victim. It is common for people to feel empathy for a person in distress and to automatically feel anger at the "abuses" he suffered. It is common to want to ease the pain and calm the person down by responding, "That's terrible. No one should have to go through what you have gone through. Something should be done about this. That person [the target, perhaps *you* who are reading this] should be punished or controlled."

Most people who know both of you are able to resist this highly emotional persuasion, but most people in court don't know either of you. First impressions can have a huge impact, and persuasive blamers are skilled at aggressively stereotyping you from the start as the evil villain.

## Negative Stereotyping

Once you, the target, are portrayed with this negative stereotype, others see you as capable of doing anything the blamer alleges. This negative stereotyping is a phenomenon researchers have studied regarding the development of racial prejudice (Carpenter 2008) and subtle influences on children's memories (Ceci and Bruck 1995).

In one study, psychologist Stephen Ceci described a man to different groups of children, with a negative stereotype to one group (the man always has accidents, breaks things). Then, that man came into the room for two minutes, walked around, and said hello and good-bye. The children were asked afterward what the man did. When the man had been described in negative terms beforehand, many of the children reported negative behaviors by him (that he threw the teddy bear and marked on it with a crayon), which had not actually occurred. They interpreted the man's neutral behavior as negative and *added events* that had never occurred but fit the stereotype. The results of the study showed that when given a negative stereotype, children will actually fabricate whole events that never occurred (ibid.).

This is similar to what happens in court with adults and even professionals when there are very few solid facts and most of the information is "he said, she said." In one custody battle in which Bill represented the mother, the father complained that the mother was dangerously inattentive to the children. He gave as an example a time when their young son and daughter had raised their voices in a brief argument in another room. The mother had not intervened, believing it was appropriate to allow the children to resolve their minor dispute themselves. Suddenly, one child had scratched the other on the face. The mother stated that there had been a "couple" of minor scratches. In his declaration, the father said the child had obtained a "few" scratches. In her court report, the court counselor stated that the child had "received twenty scratches on her face, which the mother seemed to minimize." Yet neither parent had ever said "twenty scratches." When asked in cross-examination at court where the number "twenty scratches" came from, the counselor could find nothing in her notes. She thought she had heard the father say that, but both parents agreed that he had never said that during their session, at which both had been present.

It was the counselor's error. She had formed a negative impression that the mother was irresponsible, based on the father's long list of emotional complaints, mostly of typical child behavior. Once the mother was negatively stereotyped, "events" were generated based on the emotions involved, not the evidence.

## Emotional Reasoning

A common characteristic of the cognitive distortions of people with PDs is emotional reasoning. They *feel* strongly about something and adopt "facts" to fit their feelings. They believe that the strength of their emotions proves the "truth" of the facts. These facts can be minor exaggerations, major distortions of fact to prove the opposite point, or even nonexistent events.

Because of the emotions behind them, these "emotional facts" can become very persuasive in court, especially regarding emergency orders. Bill defines emotional facts in legal cases as emotionally generated false information that is accepted as true and that appears to require emergency action. These "emotional facts" may be created unconsciously, as this excerpt from *Stop Walking on Eggshells* (Mason and Kreger 2010, 58; used with permission) aptly describes:

### Feelings Create Facts

In general, emotionally healthy people base their feelings on facts. If your dad came home drunk every night (fact), you might feel worried or concerned (feeling). If your boss complimented you on a big project (fact), you would feel proud and happy (feeling).

People with BPD, however, may do the opposite. When their feelings don't fit the facts, they may unconsciously revise the facts to fit their feelings. This may be one reason why their perspective of events is so different

from yours… [The person with borderline traits] unconsciously revises the facts so that her feelings make sense.

Some people with PDs may consciously make up events to
achieve a specific goal. Deceitfulness is one of the strongest
traits of people with antisocial personalities, as we described in
chapter 2. While their underlying distortions may be unconscious, people with antisocial personalities knowingly lie much
of the time.

> *Larry's wife wanted to gain exclusive use of the residence
> at the beginning of the divorce. This required allegations of
> abuse; otherwise, they had equal rights to stay in the house,
> pending the divorce. So Larry's wife made these allegations
> to get a "kick-out" order:*

>> *April 16,…Respondent [Larry] became angry and
>> screamed and yelled at me, following me around the
>> house, trying to pick a fight. I kept calm and appeased
>> him, and tried to keep him from becoming violent. He
>> screamed verbal abuse at me at the top of his lungs,
>> a few inches from my face…*
>>
>> *On Wednesday, April 17, at 6:15 a.m., Respondent
>> shook me violently, pushing me and shaking me
>> awake. I woke terrified…*
>>
>> *On the morning of Thursday, April 18, the
>> Respondent again yelled at me, only a few inches
>> from my face, at the top of his lungs with clenched
>> fists… I know how violent he can become, and he
>> had just pushed and shaken me the morning before…*
>>
>> *By Thursday night, Respondent had entered the
>> next stage of his anger pattern. He is silent and seeth-
>> ing. When he reaches this stage, it is only a matter
>> of time before he completely loses control and beats*

*me... Please remove Respondent from the family residence...*

This passage appears to have a great deal of credibility on the surface: it has dates and times, it shows a pattern of behavior common to the escalating cycle of domestic violence, it has descriptive detail, and most of all, it has the emotion of fear. These statements sure sound like facts.

In fact, Larry was out of state on business that week. His wife's declaration was a total fabrication. He came to court at the next full hearing with proof of his travels. His wife immediately sought to have her declaration removed from the court file and withdrew her motion for restraining orders. She had already obtained exclusive use of the residence, because the court had been convinced solely by her declaration at the first hearing (in the husband's absence, as he had not been notified because he was so "dangerous"). Larry allowed her to stay in the residence, choosing not to fight further on that issue (there were plenty more).

In reality, Larry's wife had a history of physically abusing him. She used "emotional facts," which got the quick attention of the court, yet they more aptly fit her own behavior. This projection of the PD partner's own behavior onto a target can be very powerful in court, because it has detail and raises emotional concerns. As the case progressed, it appeared that she had all three personality patterns described in this book. She repeatedly made statements to publicly destroy Larry for short-term financial gains, without empathy or remorse. Fortunately, he was able to refute every single allegation, but it took several years.

The source of emotional facts is sometimes true behavior—but someone else's behavior, not that of the target. Sometimes, blamers use true stories from the divorces of friends or others they find in the court files. When their intense emotions are added to these "facts," courts often believe them, "just to be safe." Such blamers often have ASPD or traits of ASP.

Because of their disorders, blamers have a high level of aggressive energy. While they attack their targets out of court with physical and verbal abuse, in court they repeatedly attack the target with seemingly endless allegations. The sheer number and intensity of their complaints against the target often *seem* persuasive to the court. While it will be tempting for a target to do the same, it often backfires in the long run. It's better to assertively explain patterns of the other party's harmful behavior and help the court understand that you are the reasonable party. It's always better to respond with credible information, rather than emotional appeals that are later proven to be false or exaggerated.

## Blamers Recruit Negative Advocates

Blamers tend to be ineffective problem solvers. Therefore, they seek others to solve problems for them. Rather than ask for advice and creative solutions, they seek people who will *completely agree* with their irrational beliefs and *fight for them*. These "negative advocates" may be family members, friends, professionals, or all of the above (including some lawyers and therapists). Negative advocates are people who advocate for blamers' cognitive distortions and join in their distortion campaigns against their targets. They often believe everything the blamer says about being a helpless victim and may become aggressive in trying to help. They get emotionally "hooked" into taking sides with the blamer, even though they are really uninformed about the realities of the case. Blamers lack credibility with people who really know them, but they wear down the potential advocates with their emotional intensity until they actually agree to collude with them. If enough people agree with them, it will appear to validate the blamer's beliefs.

When they go to court, the parties are allowed and encouraged to obtain declarations, investigations, evaluations, and generally the input of many people. The more witnesses, and the more credible the witnesses, the more likely you are to be believed. Therefore, blamers seek numerous and powerful advocates—especially professional advocates.

Attorneys are high on the list, because it's their role to fight for others. Many are uncritical of their clients and accept whatever they say as "just part of the job." Therapists are also sought as negative advocates, because they tend to feel empathy for and want to help those who are victims—and blamers convince others that they are victims. Sometimes neighbors and coworkers are also recruited by hearing the stories of how the blamer is a victim of the target and how the target needs to be punished in court.

Added together, these negative advocates often have a persuasive effect. Legal professionals, including judges, may think, *If this many people believe what this person is saying, it must be true.* But it often isn't true. It has little to do with the actual facts of the case (which are rarely presented to the potential negative advocate) and much more to do with the emotional intensity and "emotional facts" the blamer presents to all potential advocates. Not surprisingly, many negative advocates abandon these blamers when they become more fully informed about the blamer's behavior and the larger facts of the case. Therefore, they are always seeking and recruiting new negative advocates.

The result of this conscious or unconscious recruitment of negative advocates is that they can eventually persuade the decision makers—evaluators and judges—that *you* are doing something terrible. The focus shifts to you, rather than the blamer's own harmful behavior. With several negative advocates taking aim at you, it is very hard not to be seen as the target of the case.

## Blamers Present a False Public Persona

From a very early age, people with BP, NP, or ASP traits develop a public persona that helps them cope with their private personality distress and misbehavior. Narcissists often come to believe in their public persona: they are really cool, brilliant, powerful, well liked, and well respected. People with BP, NP, or ASP traits are able to appear calm and reasonable in public, even though they are violent and abusive at home (see Dutton 2007; Lawson 2002).

Many clients have told us that they had never seen their former partners so well behaved as when they were in court, depositions, and evaluations. They say, "He's like a whole different person, but he can't keep it up for long." The blamer has probably learned what to say and what not to say during the court process. Since, without hard facts, court can often become a battle of who *appears* most reasonable, the PD partner may really turn on the charm.

This dual personality creates special problems for targets of blame in court. When you say the blamer is an abuser, the court often discounts *your* statements because the blamer *appears* so completely reasonable. Then, when you defend yourself, you're seen as being *in denial*. The more the blamer is able to uphold his or her public persona, the less likely you will be believed, especially if you seem to be emotionally distressed and disorganized compared to the blamer's smooth public persona.

## Blamers May Do Anything to Win

Many disputes *seem* like a battle for survival to a lot of blamers because of their cognitive distortions. They feel driven to have power and control to make up for their chronic fears of abandonment, inferiority, or both. Thus, they have great difficulty with negotiating and compromising. For a person with BP traits, compromising means abandonment: "If you cared about me, we would not have to divide up our property and time with the children." For a person with NP traits, compromising means disrespect for his superiority: "If you respected me, you would let me keep all of my retirement, after all I did for you. You were nothing without me." For a person with ASP traits, compromising means a loss of dominance: "You're a mess and I know what's best for you. No one else will ever want you."

## Fantasies of Success in Court

One of the key symptoms of BPD is idealization and devaluation. Blamers expect the judge to take care of them in court, like an idealized parent who protects them, punishes others, pays a lot of sympathetic attention to them, spends a lot of time with them (their "day in court"), overlooks their faults, and generally finds in their favor.

Narcissists, especially those who are attracted to the court system, believe that they can charm anyone. They view themselves as superior and like the power that court can bestow on them.

Antisocials enjoy manipulating professionals and lying. Court may feel like a playground for them.

All of these blamers may be skilled at presenting quite an appealing and credible public persona.

## It's Easy, So Why Not?

Taking a case to court is relatively easy nowadays. While this is good for people who need the protection of the courts, it also allows or encourages people with PDs to pursue distorted beliefs or knowingly false claims. Anyone can represent himself, so a blamer doesn't have to pay for an attorney. Court filing fees can be waived if the person does not have enough money.

In many states, a majority of separating parents and divorcing parties do not use lawyers anymore.

The blamer can file papers alleging anything, and documents are readily received into the public record by the court without question. It may be weeks or months before the judge evaluates their content.

Open and equal access to our judicial system is a key element of our democratic society, but court documents must be treated with skepticism and a very open mind. From Bill's experience, declarations signed "under penalty of perjury" are often less reliable than documents written in the normal course of daily life. This is especially common with blamers, who may believe that their inaccurate statements are true. The court will weigh the credibility of each party, but it rarely specifically penalizes a party for lying.

While court personnel are not allowed to provide legal advice, most workers are helpful and often sympathetic toward people who file papers in court. This can feel very validating and encouraging to a blamer, even though it has no bearing on the final outcome of the case.

Many blamers involved in high-conflict cases obtain an attorney. Some attorneys will fight for whatever the blamer wants and will say in court whatever is requested, thus becoming negative advocates—sometimes becoming the most cynical and chronic negative advocates. But some of the nicest, most reasonable attorneys are also emotionally misled into becoming advocates for the blamer's cognitive distortions while merely trying to help.

The court will allow equal time for the blamer to say the most awful things about you in public. You can be required to miss work and spend a lot of money defending yourself, but the blamer will rarely have to compensate you for this. All the blamer has to do is make allegations, and the public will pay for investigations by Child Protective Services, the police, and possibly other public servants.

### And If the Partner with the Personality Disorder Doesn't Win?

Blamers often refuse to follow reasonable court orders. Borderline blamers *think* the court abandoned them and must have made a mistake. Narcissistic blamers *feel* that they are superior to the court's orders and superior to the judge, so the judge must have been ignorant in making this decision. They may come back to court repeatedly to try to get the judge to agree with them. They may simply ignore the court's order, or they may test the limits of the order and comply as minimally as possible.

Antisocial blamers simply *disregard* the court's orders, perhaps as a game to see what others will do, if anything. If they're caught, they will try to lie their way out of it.

Any of these blamers will search for and find loopholes in the order. In some cases, they declare bankruptcy; hide money; quit jobs; hide children; leave the state; leave the country; or make new, more dramatic and powerful allegations against you. They may try to go to another court on the same issues. They may appeal the decision. Of course, if you lose, you may want to return to court or appeal the decision, but this should be based on reason, not emotions.

# Conclusion

We hope we've neither scared you too much nor reassured you too much. The rest of the book is focused on what to do—some of it right away—now that you have an understanding of these potentially extreme patterns of behavior in a divorce process with someone who has BP, NP, or ASP traits. If you are prepared for the worst, you are less likely to be surprised, and you may have a relatively good outcome to your case. Many people have cases that can be handled completely in negotiations out of court, especially when parties and professionals know how to handle them—and the person with BP, NP, or ASP traits is less disturbed.

An increasing number of today's court cases involve severe blamers who employ the extreme measures described previously and find professionals who escalate their problems. Therefore, be prepared for the possibility that you will end up in court. You may be familiar with the behaviors previously described, or you might be very surprised at the personality that emerges from your partner in court, now that the blamer no longer believes the relationship will work out. Your partner's charm for you is usually gone by the time you enter the courthouse, but their persuasion of the court may be just beginning.

Chapter 4

# Managing a Blamer Using an Assertive Approach

After the hearing, the judge ordered Sam and Sarah into a custody evaluation and awarded Sam temporary custody of their son, Jay, pending a full evaluation and hearing on custody. Sarah was given visitation three days a week, with exchanges at her cousin's house, and required to undergo a substance-abuse assessment.

Sam also produced a deed showing that their home was in only his name, claiming it was his separate property. His attorney said that if anyone should move out, it was Sarah. He said that she could stay with her cousin. The judge seemed sympathetic with Sam and told Sarah she must move. Her temporary restraining order was dismissed.

After Tammy said that Thomas had molested their daughter, the court counselor was required by law to contact Child Protective Services (CPS) and inform them of the sexual-abuse report so that it could be investigated. To be safe, the court counselor recommended that Tammy have temporary custody and that Thomas have supervised visitation until an investigation could be done.

*Soon afterward, the court ordered a full psychological evaluation of the family and a hearing on it in three months. Until the hearing, Thomas was ordered to have three hours a week of supervised visitation at a local agency, which he had to pay for.*

*Thomas was a trusting, problem-solving person. Known as being friendly and cooperative, he originally believed he would easily succeed in his case. But after he was ordered to have supervised visitation, he was furious with his attorney: "How could the judge assume I'm guilty and make such an order? Why didn't you tell the court Tammy was lying? If she's going to make a bunch of allegations, then we need to make even more allegations against her."*

*His attorney responded, "Slow down. This is just the beginning. We can't be passive, but we can't be too aggressive either. This is the court's procedure, and we need to follow it as perfectly as we can. We have to take the high road and expose her false statements while not appearing to make wild accusations ourselves. How you appear to the court is just as important as getting out the facts. We now have a lot of work to do to accomplish both. We have to be very assertive."*

In the last two chapters we gave you *knowledge* about people with BP, NP, and ASP traits and how they engage in extreme, but predictable, patterns of blaming behavior. Now, we want to help you focus your *energy* on what is important in your case and help you avoid wasting energy by overreacting unnecessarily to certain behaviors you can ignore. The assertive approach gives you energy, which is the first "E" in the acronym KEEP CALM described in chapter 1.

# Not Walking on Eggshells

Family court presents a difficult dilemma for reasonable people. If you act reasonably and use the cooperative problem-solving skills you use in daily life, you risk losing your case, because family court is a highly adversarial process that rewards combative thinking and behavior. This is why people with BP, NP, and ASP traits are often attracted to court and often win.

If you take a passive approach—and many do—then the blamer's allegations appear unchallenged and therefore true. Sarah allowed this to happen at her hearing, when she did not have an attorney and did not respond in her own defense to Sam's allegations. If you allow this to happen, it gets harder and harder to overcome the appearance that you *accept* the allegations as true. Remember, the burden is on you (and your attorney) to assert your position. The court won't otherwise try to figure it out, and rarely asks you questions, such as whether or not you agree. You or your attorney must convey assertively that you *do not agree*; otherwise, the judge may assume that each of the blamer's statements is true.

But if your approach is too aggressive, you may give the appearance of being the abusive person you say that you're not. Thomas's urge to have his attorney make a lot of unsupported allegations against Tammy at the next hearing will generally backfire. While TV and movies are filled with dramatic and aggressive attorneys, a tactic of aggression often backfires in real courts, especially in the long run. Court research shows that lawyers who use an assertive approach are equally as effective with the outcome of the case as ones who use an aggressive approach, even though the aggressive attorneys may appear more successful on the surface (Rieke and Stutman 1990). Ultimately, most court cases are won or lost based on the evidence gathered through assertive homework. In reality, in family court, the burden is on you to raise credible reports of abuse you or your children have experienced or to respond to false abuse allegations against you. You and your attorney must be very assertive about gathering evidence that already exists, presenting that evidence to the court, and noticing new evidence as it occurs throughout your case.

## The Assertive Approach

**Start documenting right away.** High-conflict divorces often start with an emergency court hearing about true or false allegations of abusive behavior. If you or the person with BP, NP, or ASP traits is seeking court orders (often restraining or "protective" orders), it is critical that you put together detailed, accurate information to present to the court.

Somewhere in a safe place, record detailed information about parenting behavior (yours and the other parent's), abusive behaviors, threatening statements made, and explanations of any confrontations between the two of you. Many people keep a daily diary, even before they separate. Focus on actual statements and behaviors, and avoid opinions and interpretations. If you need to describe events in court, you want to be seen as capable of presenting very objective, factual information that's most helpful to the judge and other professionals. Information that is written down the day of the event is considered far more credible than something written a week or a month later.

**Think strategically, not reactively.** Avoid acting out of frustration and anger; otherwise, you may do things that waste energy and will hurt you in the long term, as Thomas did (just once) before he learned the consequences.

*Thomas was so upset after the hearing in which supervised visitation was ordered for him that he sent Tammy an email saying that she should be ashamed of herself and that their daughter would never forgive her for lying and saying he abused her. At the next hearing, this spontaneous and reactive email showed up as an exhibit to Tammy's declaration, intended to show that Thomas was aggressive, angry, and unstable. Thomas's lawyer convinced him to never send Tammy an angry email again without showing it to him first.*

It's important to avoid reacting and communicating with the other person without advice. "Stop and think" are some of the most important words when you enter a family court battle.

Check with a therapist or an attorney whenever you feel like communicating angrily with your partner. You are better off processing your frustrations in therapy than putting something angry in writing or in a voice mail that could inadvertently become a new court document. Advise your friends and relatives to avoid such angry statements to your partner for the same reason.

**Choose your battles.** Many people who are divorcing someone with BP, NP, or ASP traits complain about how unfair the court process is and how unfair it is that the blamer gets away with certain things. Of course this is upsetting, but your case actions must be based on what you need to do to make it right, not what you feel upset about. You must think strategically and choose your battles.

Talk to your attorney about which issues need a response and which ones you can ignore. Letters from your partner's attorney to your attorney can be very provocative but don't always need a response, especially if they are not in the court record. "Your client is always late with support payments and doesn't seem to care if the children ever eat again"—this letter may not need a response at all. To respond is a choice. If there was a problem and the payment was a day or two late, it may help to provide an explanation to the blamer's attorney, just in case this letter shows up as an exhibit to a declaration at the next hearing.

You should always respond to court declarations containing false statements. A general denial may be sufficient, but false information in court needs a written correction, just to protect you now and in the future.

**Don't make yourself into a target.** When you're in a family court battle, you need to be as perfect as possible. Stop and think as often as you can. Remember, you're being watched by your partner and your partner's attorney. Any of your public actions and some of your private actions may be exposed and twisted around to fit their adversarial purposes.

Innocent discussions with your partner, or even your partner's relatives or friends, may get blown out of proportion. Just when everything seems to be going well, you may be caught by surprise and find some innocent action held against you. The ironic saying "No good deed goes unpunished" seems to really fit in family courts.

Stop and think about how your parenting decisions and actions could be interpreted by your partner's attorney, a court evaluator, or the judge. Check questionable practices with your lawyer, such as the following:

*Target:*    My five-year-old daughter shared a bed with me last weekend at my new apartment. Is that okay?

*Attorney:*  No. Get a bed for her immediately, or else you'll be accused of sexual abuse.

*Target:*    I need to pay some bills, so I'm going to pay the child support a few days late. Is that okay?

*Attorney:*  No. Pay it before everything else, or it will cost you dearly in the long run in court. Judges see child support as sacred.

*Target:*    I'm afraid my husband will spend everything in our savings account, so I'm going to transfer it all to an account in only my name. Okay?

*Attorney:*    No. Take half, at most, or you'll be blamed for raiding his share of the funds.

Another way to avoid becoming a target is to keep a low profile on the internet during your divorce. Many lawyers recommend that you temporarily shut down any social networking pages you have with public profiles but don't permanently delete any files. These pages are often used in family court as evidence of bad behavior. On the other hand, you might look for information about the other person. The best example we've heard is the recovering alcoholic who said he hadn't had a drink in years. At the same time, he had an online photo that was captioned, "Me at Last Week's Party," with him and his buddies—and a bottle of beer in his hand! This is great evidence for court. Likewise, social networking websites may be a fast way to communicate with friends, but they can also be a fast way to make a mistake. Be very careful what you publish to the world.

**Be very honest.** Admit your own errors and poor judgment to your attorney as soon as you recognize them so that your attorney can prepare a response, if necessary. Remember, you're a target. Your partner will blame you, possibly investigate you, and misinterpret you. Things that are half true are harder to deny than statements you can prove to be totally false.

*Sarah had a history of lying to cover up Sam's physical abuse of her. This is common and certainly understandable. But then Sam's sister submitted a declaration that said that Sarah had claimed she had hurt herself through her own clumsiness. Sarah's attorney will need to explain this to the court and possibly have an expert testify that covering up the abuse is common in domestic violence cases. But these lies can't be ignored, or they will be used to attack Sarah's credibility later on.*

Credibility is everything in court. Blamers are generally better at *appearing* credible in court, so judges believe them instead of you. Blamers are more emotional in a focused manner, and research has shown that emotions are contagious (Goleman 2006). Emotions get the judge's attention and can motivate action, but unfocused emotions can backfire, so don't count on using emotional persuasion yourself.

Your best defense is to be completely honest. If you have made a false statement, acknowledge it as soon as possible. If you catch the other person making false statements and you have been honest, you may ultimately win your case. Since the blamer will appear more credible, you have to be more credible.

**Expose blamer behavior.** Interestingly, blamers create some of the most useful evidence during their court cases. Remember, they have patterns of behavior that keep repeating even when they should be more careful, because they can't stop themselves. Be prepared to take the initiative in showing the court the blamer's true behavior patterns.

*Tammy did everything she could to interfere with Thomas's supervised visits with their daughter. "Brianna doesn't feel comfortable seeing Thomas at all," she said to the supervisor before the first visit, asking if it could be canceled. Then she came up with, "Brianna doesn't feel comfortable with the visitation supervisor anymore," after the supervisor seemed too friendly with Thomas. Later she stated, "I'm not bringing Brianna for the scheduled time this week because it interferes with a weekend trip I need to take to see my parents."*

*After carefully documenting these attempts to interfere with Thomas's visits with his daughter, his attorney scheduled an emergency ex parte hearing to make sure Tammy did not interfere further with the supervised visitation schedule. He pointed out her aggressive behavior and Thomas's fully cooperative behavior, stating, "The supervisor says that Brianna is always eager to see her father."*

*The judge said, "If that's true, then ask the supervisor to write a report saying that. I find that very interesting. And you, ma'am, need to stop interfering with his visits. It makes me wonder what's really going on here."*

Usually blamers try to control the entire court process themselves or through their lawyers. They make dramatic statements at each hearing and usually ask for heavy controls to be placed on their partners because of their alleged "abusive behavior." Their extreme statements at each hearing can be very useful in showing the court later on that they are false. The first hearing often provides you with some of the best evidence in your case. The blamer and his lawyer are often overconfident and feel that their allegations will catch you by surprise at first and sway the court.

Make sure that a court reporter is typing all of these statements, if possible, then get a copy of the court transcript. At a later hearing, if there are statements that were made that were false, you can provide evidence of that and show a pattern of false statements made to the judge (see chapter 14). Judges really dislike being lied to, and catching lies during the case may have a powerful impact on the court. Taking depositions of blamers, and their various advocates, can often show numerous other false or contradictory statements, which help demonstrate to the judge a pattern of behavior that won't stop without the court's intervention.

**Respond quickly.** A blamer's false statements and extreme actions generally need your quick response. Otherwise, it seems as if you agree that they were true statements and appropriate actions. As shown in the last example, by responding quickly, Thomas and his attorney were able to show Tammy's behavior while it was happening. If you respond quickly, the blamer and her attorney learn that aggressive or inappropriate actions will receive a rapid response, which may slow down or stop some of this behavior. If you fight back assertively, the blamer will usually back off, give up, or target someone else.

If you put everything into assertively fighting back and preparing for court from the start of your case, you may never have to be a target again.

## Assertively Selecting Your Divorce Method

Throughout the divorce process, use your assertiveness skills to choose the appropriate setting for your divorce. As we describe in part 3 of this book, there are many options for resolving your divorce totally out of court. Propose using these methods to save both of you time, money, and stress. Throughout the divorce process, keep suggesting out-of-court solutions, but prepare for a court battle. From time to time, you may need to switch your strategy, given the possibilities and realities. You want to make sure your strategy takes into account whether the other party is a mild, moderate, or severe blamer, and you may not know this until you're in the middle of the process.

## Emotional Aspects of the Assertive Approach

**Manage your own emotions.** Dealing with someone with BP, NP, or ASP traits can be extremely difficult, especially when the person's behavior has escalated and her blame of you is extreme. You will frequently get emotionally hooked into wanting to respond aggressively or giving up. This is natural because, as we said, a blamer's emotional intensity is contagious. But you will be most successful if you can first discuss your responses with your therapist or attorney and then keep a matter-of-fact tone of voice with the blamer. You will need to pace yourself to conserve your energy for the important battles, not for every little zinger your partner throws at you.

People with BP, NP, or ASP traits are generally more comfortable dealing on a highly emotional level. If you engage them by responding at a highly emotional level, things almost always escalate. Since your partner will have great difficulty managing his own emotions, he will overreact to you. So, don't overreact in response and add to the escalation. Instead, practice responding in a matter-of-fact way and then getting out of the conversation without insulting or blatantly rejecting your partner.

**Your emotions are also contagious.** Neuroscientists have said for years that emotions are contagious. Then they discovered mirror neurons, which may explain why. We actually mirror in our brains what other people are doing while we are watching them. These neurons apparently help us prepare to engage in similar actions. When someone is angry, we automatically start preparing our mouths, hands, and bodies to behave in the same way. When someone is smiling, we have an urge to smile back (Iacoboni 2008).

With this in mind, *your* emotions are also contagious. Avoid mirroring back your partner's upset or otherwise inappropriate emotions. Avoid trying to talk him out of his emotions or cognitive distortions. Instead, simply respond with your own moderate emotions ("That's interesting," "I'll think about that," "Thanks for considering my proposal"), and your partner may mirror you. This may help your partner calm herself down, even when things are difficult. Of course, don't rely on this if you need to protect yourself by having minimal contact or no direct contact, especially in cases with a history of domestic violence.

**Develop patience and flexibility.** An important part of the assertive approach is calmly showing patience and flexibility, something that's the opposite of what you may feel, so it may take some practice. You can discuss this with a therapist or an attorney and even role-play conversations with one of these professionals before you actually discuss the matter with your partner.

Allow some time for your partner to process upsetting information. Avoid presenting information or a decision as a crisis that has to be resolved instantly. Since your partner will often overreact at first, suggest that he take time to think about a new idea or a change in your life (but don't say why you're doing this). This is especially true before taking one of the actions described in chapter 3 as "Key Times of Risk of Extreme Behavior." Say, "Next week, my lawyer will be sending you some papers for a court hearing about our parenting plan and child support. Please take your time to think about these matters, and let me know if you think we could reach an agreement before the hearing. Then the hearing won't be necessary. Or, we can just let the judge decide."

Giving a heads-up and showing your flexibility will reduce the sense of a threat so that extreme behavior is less likely to be triggered. This can be especially important if there have already been many recent losses in the person's life. Showing some patience, empathy, and respect can help people who are upset have some hope in their lives. Of course, prepare yourself for a fully upset response at any time, regardless of what you do. (In some situations, such as seeking an emergency restraining order, it may be beneficial to avoid advance notice, for safety reasons.)

It's common for someone with BP, NP, or ASP traits to feel that she is in a crisis and want you to make a decision instantly. Don't buy into this. You can always say, "Give me time to think about it. I'm inclined to say no, but I'll get back to you in two days." In other words, don't absorb your partner's crisis. Just calmly turn it into another problem to solve. This buys you time to get consultation if you need it or time just to calm down and think it through. This also gives your partner an opportunity to calm down and lower his expectations because you already said you're not inclined to do it.

**Give clear messages and deadlines.** The assertive approach works only if you balance your patience and flexibility with clear messages and deadlines. Otherwise, the person with BP, NP, or ASP traits will walk all over you. This is common for many targets who overemphasize patience and flexibility. (The assertive approach only works if you balance clear messages and deadlines with patience and flexibility; otherwise, you will be too aggressive.)

As much as possible, don't convey emotional ambivalence if you're not ambivalent. Give clear messages. Otherwise, the person with BP, NP, or ASP traits will have unrealistic hopes and put a lot of energy into trying to get you to change your mind—especially about the whole separation and divorce.

Many people with BP traits keep trying to talk their partners back into a relationship months or even years after the separation and divorce. Unless this is a realistic possibility, don't reinforce this thinking at all. Patience means allowing time for the other person to adjust. Flexibility means there's room to negotiate the details. None of this means you will change your mind about ending the marriage or taking the actions necessary to move the divorce forward.

When necessary, give a deadline for responding to your questions, requests, or proposals. You don't have to start out with that, but you can add that later if there's no response. You or your lawyer might put in writing: "Two weeks ago, I sent you a letter with several proposals for the division of our property. Since we haven't heard back from you, we are now requesting a response within the next ten days. If we hear no response by that date, we will need to file for a trial on these issues. I hope that won't be necessary."

This way, you're not giving up all your power just because you're open to negotiating. In cases with mild blamers, you might try negotiations first before filing for a hearing or trial. In cases with severe blamers, it often helps to file for a hearing or trial and then offer to engage in negotiations—with the hearing or trial date as a deadline. It's common for people with narcissistic or antisocial traits to not respond at all to settlement proposals unless there is a deadline with a real consequence (like having the judge decide the issues with a less-favorable outcome).

**Remember BIFF when responding to hostile emails.** The text box describes an assertive approach you can use for responding to hostile emails that's neither aggressive nor passive.

## BIFF Communications

Hostile texts and email exchanges have become huge in divorce. Blamers love sending them and use them to attack you, your family and friends, and professionals. It's extremely tempting to respond in kind. Hostile email has also become huge in family court, as a document used to show someone's bad behavior. While you are encouraged to save copies of hostile emails sent to you, it is very important that you not send hostile emails to anyone. They will be used against you. Instead, assertively use a BIFF response, as described next, and encourage people in your support system to do the same. It will save you a lot of wasted time and energy to be *brief, informative, friendly,* and *firm.*

**Do you need to respond?** Much hostile mail does not need a response. Letters from exes, angry neighbors, irritating coworkers, or attorneys do not usually have legal significance.

The letter itself has no power, unless you give it power. Often, it is emotional venting aimed at relieving the writer's anxiety. If you respond with similar emotions and hostility, you will simply escalate things without satisfaction and just get a new piece of hostile mail back. In most cases, you are better off not responding. Some letters and emails develop power when copies are filed in a court or complaint process—or simply get sent to other people. In these cases, it may be important to respond to inaccurate statements with accurate statements of fact. If so, use a BIFF response.

### Brief

Keep your response brief. This will reduce the chances of a prolonged and angry back-and-forth. The more you write, the more material the other person has to criticize. Keeping it brief signals that you don't wish to engage in a dialogue. Just make your response and end your email. Don't take your partner's statements personally, and don't respond with a personal attack. Avoid focusing on comments about the other person's character, such as saying he is rude, insensitive, or stupid. It just escalates the conflict and keeps it going. Make sure to avoid the three "A's": admonishments, advice, and apologies. You don't have to defend yourself to someone you disagree with. If your friends still like you, you don't have to prove anything to people who don't.

### Informative

The main reason to respond to hostile mail is to correct inaccurate statements others might see. "Just the facts" is a good thing to keep in mind. Focus on the accurate statements you want to make, not on the inaccurate statements the other person made: "Just to clear things up, I was out of town on February 12, so I would not have been the person who was making loud noises that day."

Avoid negative comments, sarcasm, and threats. Avoid personal remarks about the other person's intelligence, ethics, or moral behavior. If the other person has a high-conflict personality, you will have no success at reducing the conflict by making personal attacks. While most people can ignore personal attacks or might think harder about what you are saying, high-conflict people feel they have no choice but to respond in anger—and keep the conflict going. Personal attacks rarely lead to insight or positive change.

### Friendly

While you may be tempted to write in anger, you are more likely to achieve your goals by writing in a friendly manner. Consciously thinking about a friendly response will increase your chances of getting a friendly or neutral response in return. If your goal is to end the conflict, then being friendly has the greatest likelihood of success. Don't give the other person a reason to get defensive and keep responding. This does not mean that you have to be overly friendly. Just make your message sound a little relaxed and nonantagonistic. If appropriate, say you recognize your partner's concerns. Brief comments that show your empathy and respect will generally calm the other person down, even if only for a short time.

### Firm

In a nonthreatening way, clearly tell the other person your information or position on an issue, such as, "That's all I'm going to say on this issue." Be careful not to make comments that invite more discussion, unless you are negotiating an issue or want to keep a dialogue going. Avoid comments that leave an opening, such as "I hope you will agree with me that…" This invites the other person to tell you, "I *don't* agree."

Sound confident and don't ask for more information, if you want to end the back-and-forth. A confident-sounding person is less likely to be challenged with further emails. If you get more emails, you can ignore them, if you have already sufficiently addressed the inaccurate information. If you need to respond again, keep it even briefer, and do not emotionally engage. In fact, it often helps to just repeat the key information using the same words.

### Example of BIFF Response

Joe's hostile email:

*Jane, I can't believe you are so stupid as to think I'm going to let you take the children to your boss's birthday party during my parenting time. Have you no memory of the last six conflicts we've had about my parenting time? Or are you having an affair with him? I always knew you would do anything to get ahead! In fact, I remember coming to your office party and witnessing you making a total fool of yourself, including flirting with everyone from the CEO down to the mailroom clerk! Are you high on something? Haven't you gotten your finances together enough to support yourself yet, without flinging yourself at every Tom, Dick, and Harry?...*

Jane's response:

*Thank you for responding to my request to take the children to my office party. Just to clarify, the party will be from 3:00 to 5:00 on Friday at the office, and there will be approximately thirty people there, including several other parents and their school-age children. There will be*

*no alcohol because it is a family-oriented*
*firm, and there will be family-oriented*
*activities. I think it will be a good expe-*
*rience for the kids to see me at my work-*
*place. Since you do not agree, then, of*
*course, I will respect that and withdraw*
*my request, because I recognize that it is*
*your parenting time.*

Jane kept it brief and did not engage in defending herself. Since this was just between the two of them, she didn't need to respond. If he sent this email to friends, coworkers, or family members (which high-conflict people often do), she would need to respond to the larger group with more information, such as the following.

Jane's group response:    *Dear friends and family,*
*As you know, Joe and I had a diffi-*
*cult divorce. He has sent you a private*
*email showing correspondence between*
*us about a parenting schedule matter. I*
*hope you will see this as a private matter*
*and understand that you do not need to*
*respond or get involved in any way. If*
*you have any questions for me person-*
*ally, please feel free to contact me and I*
*will clarify anything I can. I appreciate*
*your friendship and support.*

And that's BIFF: brief, informative, friendly, and firm! (Eddy et al. 2020)

For more examples of BIFF communications see the books *BIFF: Quick Responses to High Conflict People* (2nd Edition, Unhooked Books, 2014) and *BIFF for CoParent Communication* (Unhooked Books, 2020).

## Evidence of Communications

In high-conflict cases, it often helps to have a mechanism for collecting electronic communications, so that both parties know that what they say may be seen in court someday. This often gets better behavior from someone with a PD or traits. One such method is Our Family Wizard, which is a subscription computer system that is organized to save your communications, including schedules and expenses.

Another such method is PwrSwitch, which helps you easily retrieve previous emails and texts, and phone call dates and times (not conversations).

Our PatternViewer method organizes electronic communications, as well as other documents (letters, reports, etc.), so they can be organized to show patterns of concerning behavior and easily presented to decision makers.

All of these methods are described in more depth on this book's webpage with the publisher (see Resources at the back of this book).

# Conclusion

This chapter has given you an assertive approach for dealing with a partner with BP, NP, or ASP traits in any divorce. This assertive approach emphasizes focusing on factual information rather than emotional responses, and responding quickly to the many allegations that a blamer may make against you. Determining whether you can resolve your case out of court versus in court is rarely clear-cut, so keep making out-of-court proposals while preparing for court along the way. Think of using your assertiveness skills as an ongoing process that will save you energy by focusing your energy.

# Chapter 5

# Preparing for a Court Battle with a Blamer

*Sarah was not used to fighting for herself. She did not look forward to a court battle with Sam. She knew she would have to bring out the history of his abuse against her and their son, Jay. She also hoped they could just settle their case out of court. She was so overwhelmed that she didn't know what to expect or what to do. Her attorney suggested that they consider settling some issues out of court while preparing for court. But most of all, Sarah needed to prepare herself to have energy for the ups and downs of a difficult divorce. To get Sarah ready, her attorney suggested she take several steps to build her confidence, get support, and warn others of what might be ahead.*

## Three Divorce Scenarios

There are three general scenarios for resolving divorces involving a partner with BP, NP, or ASP traits, depending on the severity of the person's personality traits. Sarah may spend her whole case in court, but some issues may be settled out of court, such as the division of the property she and Sam own together. Your case may not involve domestic violence or a severe BP, NP, or ASP blamer. Therefore, we want you to know about all three divorce possibilities before preparing you for the worst-case scenario of a court battle.

You should always be prepared for a court battle to avoid being caught by surprise if your case suddenly escalates and you end up in court with a blamer. We have seen this over and over again. In part 2 we focus on how to manage such a court battle, and in part 3 we discuss the alternatives to litigation.

The following chart gives an overview of the three most common scenarios for any divorce, including those involving a partner with BP, NP, or ASP traits. Terms on the chart vary by state, but the steps are similar. The details are referred to occasionally in this book, so you might place a bookmark on this page for easy reference.

## Three Divorce Scenarios with a Borderline, Narcissistic, or Antisocial Partner

| Mild Cases (No court hearings) | Moderate Cases (One to two court hearings) | Severe Cases (Many hearings and trial) |
|---|---|---|
| 1. Petition filed<br><br>• Settlement discussions | 1. Petition filed<br><br>• File for temporary hearing on custody, visitation, child support, and spousal support | 1. Petition filed<br><br>• Emergency court hearing: restraining orders, restricted visitation, residence exclusion, or some combination<br><br>• File for temporary hearing on custody, visitation, child support, and spousal support |

| Mild Cases (No court hearings) | Moderate Cases (One to two court hearings) | Severe Cases (Many hearings and trial) |
|---|---|---|
| 2. Exchange of information | 2. Exchange of information | 2. Exchange of information |
| • Share financial data and parenting information | • File declarations for hearing, start settlement discussions | • File declarations and documents for hearings |
| • Two to four settlement discussions in mediation, collaborative divorce, attorney negotiations, or settlement without any professionals | • Some issues settled, but one or two temporary hearings on unresolved issues | • Get evaluator appointed, prepare documents for evaluators and court |
| • Reach full agreement | • Possible evaluator agreed on for parenting or financial issues in dispute | • Serve subpoenas, take depositions, demand documents |
| | • Temporary hearings, evaluation, or both reduce parties' expectations and narrow issues | • Attend numerous temporary hearings |
| | • Numerous settlement negotiations between attorneys, parties, or both | |
| | • Reach full agreement on all issues | |

| Mild Cases (No court hearings) | Moderate Cases (One to two court hearings) | Severe Cases (Many hearings and trial) |
|---|---|---|
| 3. Divorce judgment<br>• Write up marital settlement agreement<br>• Have agreement filed at court and approved by judge | 3. Divorce judgment<br>• Many drafts of marital settlement agreement, finally approved by all, filed at court, approved by judge | 3. Divorce judgment<br>• Trial, with delays, disputes over evaluators' reports, and other objections<br>• Disputes over trial court's orders, motions for reconsideration, appeals, and so forth |
|  |  | 4. Postdivorce hearings<br>• Modifications of support, custody battles<br>• New or failed relationships cause renewed conflicts |

© 2004 by Bill Eddy.

In general, you don't give up your rights to go to court if you attempt to settle the issues in your case out of court. You can always go to court if settlement efforts fail, but the decision to use an alternative to court must be made jointly by the parties, which is often unlikely when a blamer is involved. Some people with BP, NP, or ASP traits are able to resolve their divorces out of court if their professionals can shift them from blame to compromise.

The amount of court involvement is determined not only by the severity of a partner's BP, NP, or ASP traits but also by the negative or positive actions of the person's various advocates (lawyers, counselors, family, and friends). We encourage you to try an out-of-court approach from the beginning of the case, if you can.

Your blamer may be interested, especially because it can save money. He may assume that you won't contest his proposals. Your blamer may decide she wants to go to court to have someone else make the decisions. In fact, your blamer may have you served with papers and may force you to go to court, whether or not you prefer an alternative method to resolve your differences. It takes two to stay out of court. Of course, you may need court orders to have the blamer restrained from certain conduct, to protect the children from the blamer, or both.

In general, you should prepare for the adversarial process much more than someone who's going to court over a purely legal issue. Expect that the blamer will escalate the case to a much higher emotional level than most court cases and that the person's cognitive distortions will confuse or mislead many of the professionals involved in your case, whether you resolve it in or out of court.

# Focus Your Energy

You may potentially face a high-conflict court battle that may involve numerous allies and enemies on both sides. Following are some recommendations to help you focus your energy for all scenarios, which will also give you more energy.

## Get Lots of Personal Support

This is not a time to walk on eggshells. Rather, this is a time to have a support system in place with knowledgeable and caring friends, family members, and professionals. It is harder to undo bad court orders than to confront issues as hard as you can early on. For this you will need a strong and knowledgeable support system to give you energy. This is essential, because the court process can drain you emotionally, financially, and timewise even if you're prepared for it.

## How Family and Friends Can Help

You will need several people to talk to as the going gets tough. Make them aware that you may become a temporary "basket case" if the escalating court conflict takes over your life. They need to know that this is normal in these cases, and they can imagine their role as like sending you off into battle and patching you up when you come back.

Family and friends often have resources, perspective, ideas, and energy that you may not have. They can help by researching subjects online, making phone calls, going to bookstores, and asking around for information when you are at work or feel overwhelmed. Often family and friends may know of professionals, books, programs, support groups, therapists, and other services that might be available but unknown to you. For over a decade, many people have reported blaming themselves for their partner's moody and extreme behavior until they heard about Randi's book *Stop Walking on Eggshells*, mostly through word of mouth from family and friends.

## Do You Need a Therapist?

Yes! Find a therapist who understands borderline, narcissistic, and antisocial personalities to help you prepare for the bumpy (but predictable) road ahead and to help you manage your own emotions when you are blamed for one issue after another. Begin meeting with a therapist before starting the court process, if possible. A therapist can help you:

- Process and manage your own feelings

- Look for cognitive distortions in your own thinking (*I know I'll lose; I'm helpless*)

- Predict possible extreme behavior by your blamer at key times

- Develop realistic expectations of court

- Cope with grief when there are losses along the way

- Put the court battle into the larger context of your life

- Develop realistic expectations of a child's developmental needs

- Learn stress-reduction techniques

A therapist can help you understand and remember your goals, which you may otherwise easily get distracted from in the heat of battle. You'll need the therapist's knowledgeable support and a safe place to handle the fear and anger triggered by the court process. In some cases, a therapist may write a declaration on your behalf, speak credibly with a court-appointed expert, help you psychologically prepare for giving court testimony, or do all of these.

We have learned over many years that targets are more likely to use therapists and more likely to reflect on their own behavior than blamers. Therefore, you may have an advantage in court by having a therapist. This is because the court may see you as more interested in taking responsibility and working on yourself, while the blamer more often doesn't have a therapist and doesn't want to look at changing anything.

An alternative is to seek a divorce coach. This person can help you with some of the specific tasks of dealing with your divorce without focusing as much on your personal growth and emotional needs. Some mental health professionals who have been trained in collaborative divorce may offer services as a divorce coach, even to those who are not involved in collaborative divorce.

In Bill's most difficult, but successful, cases, his clients started working with a therapist early in the case. The therapist was able to help a client keep calm; explain personality-disordered behavior to the client; develop strategies for dealing with the partner with BP, NP, or ASP traits; and communicate with Bill about issues and ideas as they prepared for court. A therapist can help, even if you only see the professional occasionally.

## Do You Need a Divorce Financial Analyst?

There are many financial issues involved in a divorce case, and even in unmarried cases with children there are financial questions related to child support and each party's income. Therefore, it is recommended that you at least consult with a certified divorce financial analyst. They are experienced in all of the financial issues, from incomes, to property division, to planning for your future needs. Especially because of the manipulations of a blamer, you may find it very helpful to have someone who can figure out what is really going on.

## Get Financial Support

Gather the funds necessary to afford an attorney, a therapist or coach, possibly an investigator, and various other experts who could be needed or ordered by the court. Some people take out a loan or borrow from their retirement savings; others use a credit card. It's difficult to estimate the cost of your case. Your primary cost will be attorney fees. Rates vary greatly around the country, but it's not unusual today for family-law attorney fees to range from two hundred fifty to five hundred dollars per hour, depending on your geographic area (higher on the

East and West coasts), the attorney's years of experience, and the number of hearings involved in your case—which is often determined by how driven the blamer is to bring issues to court, large and small. You should have access to at least five to ten thousand dollars to be ready to start a very assertive approach to handling your case.

If the blamer makes false allegations, you may need to spend money responding to them and having evaluations conducted to prove that you did not do what you're accused of doing. This can include the cost of a court-appointed psychological evaluator and your own psychological expert in parenting disputes. In financial disputes, this can include a court-appointed forensic accountant or special master, plus your own private financial advisor. You may need to hire an investigator and obtain substantial records. In most cases, the parties pay the cost of all the professionals involved in a court battle.

In many cases, the party who has the greater income may be ordered by the court to pay more of these costs for both of you, to equalize both parties' access to attorneys and other experts. But before you get to court, your blamer may block your access to funds that are rightfully yours. Therefore, check with an attorney about how to set aside some funds before you separate if possible, in a manner that does not violate your local laws. In some states you can retain an attorney with savings that were earned by either party during the marriage. But after you file your petition opening a legal case, there may be requirements restricting your movement of funds any further.

Many people pay their fees by credit card, borrow from their retirement savings, or borrow from relatives in order to fully respond to whatever the blamer does from the start. Attorneys usually take an up-front retainer. If you want your attorney to be focused on fighting hard, you won't want this professional to be distracted by worries about getting paid.

## Representing Yourself

In more and more cases, people are representing themselves in family court these days. In this case, you are still encouraged to at least consult with a lawyer for an hour at the beginning, and possibly ongoing, for tips on legal standards, court rules, and dealing with a difficult person on the other side. More lawyers are willing to assist like this and more judges understand that you will represent yourself.

Find out if your court has special forms, procedures, and any assistance for unrepresented parties. Go to the court and sit in on some hearings, if you can. Ideally, find out which courtroom and judge are involved in your case and watch some court hearings before you prepare for yours. Some courts have office staff to answer some procedural questions, but not to give legal advice. While you may feel confident in your ability to handle a court hearing on your own, consider the possibility that your blamer and his or her lawyer may try to destroy you in court. When a blamer is involved, it is rarely just a routine matter that you can easily handle yourself.

## Consult with Experts

Courts often order experts to be involved in today's cases as neutral evaluators, because judges don't have the time or background knowledge to resolve these cases on their own. Psychologists commonly serve as evaluators in the types of cases raised by blamers (child abuse, domestic violence, and so forth), but sometimes the conflicts are over finances, so a CPA (certified public accountant) might become involved. Also, an attorney for children or a guardian ad litem may be appointed in custody and visitation disputes.

Before an evaluator is appointed by the court, it helps to consult with a mental health professional, financial adviser, or other professional who is familiar with the way the court handles the issues potentially involved in your case in your county. Family law issues involve state laws, which are interpreted primarily at the county level by individual judges. Therefore, you're best served by finding someone knowledgeable about your specific county and your specific judge, if possible.

You don't necessarily need to retain an expert before you go to court. But see if you can find someone you can meet at least once before your case really begins. After your case gets going, you will see whether it escalates into a full court battle requiring experts or whether it settles down and experts are not required. At least you will be prepared after meeting an expert.

# Warn Employers and Others to Be Prepared

Blamers often contact numerous people in their distortion campaigns. It's common for them to contact your employer, your grandparents, your accountant, your doctor, your minister, your children, and others to complain about you and your "awful" behavior by exaggerating, distorting, or outright fabricating tales of events. At best, blamers hope to win sympathy. At worst, they hope to turn others against you.

Tip off important people in your life as soon as possible. Let them know that you're entering a legal battle and that your soon-to-be ex (don't label the person as having a PD) may try to persuade those closest to you to join in blaming you for some unknown and often made-up behavior. Encourage others to remain open-minded and cautious in forming opinions. Ask them to call you if they have any questions or doubts raised by rumors of your alleged actions, before they make assumptions or take sides.

Blamers often start the case against the target by taking extreme legal action. You may be served with court papers (often restraining orders) at your place of work by a marshal or two. This is totally legal, but rarely necessary. Your friends and relatives may suddenly turn cold toward you, as they try to avoid getting caught in the conflict, or they may get emotionally hooked by the blamer's stories.

In one case, a blamer mother told relatives a variety of tall tales about the target father, including allegations of domestic violence, child sexual abuse, stealing family money, lying to relatives, and so forth to see which allegations got the most response. The domestic violence allegations seemed to get the most attention from relatives, so that's what the blamer took to court. The allegations were eventually determined to be unfounded.

In another case, after the target mother moved out of the area following the divorce, a blamer father repeatedly called her new place of employment to find out her work hours, the length of her contract, her benefits, and so forth. Each time, he spoke to a different person and asked for different information, explaining that he was her ex-husband and needed to know this detailed information. It gave him a sense of superiority (narcissistic personality?) that he could cause concern about her, but it eventually put her job at risk.

What he should have done was sent a formal request through his attorney to her attorney to obtain the information. But gaining information was not his goal; his goal was to harass and intimidate her. Once she explained to her employer that the company had no obligation to talk to him, the problem was solved.

## Possibly Notify Law Enforcement

Some targets report success with filing an information report with the local police department warning of a potential false allegation of child abuse or domestic violence. Then, if there is a 911 call, the police will already know it might be false and the result of a personality problem instead of actual abuse, and they will be open-minded as they investigate.

If you're the victim of domestic violence or your children are the victims of child abuse by the other parent, you may also want to discuss these problems with law enforcement. After all, there are some antisocial blamers who will make false allegations that you will make false allegations of abuse, thereby covering themselves when they do abuse you in the future. Partners with antisocial personality traits are the most devious planners of all, and some of them particularly enjoy conning the police and legal professionals.

If any incidents of violence occur against you or your children, it's important to write down what happened and to seek professional involvement as soon as possible, whether in the form of law enforcement or medical assistance. Many targets are afraid to let others know that they have been abused, but it is this silence and secretiveness that allows it to continue. Don't resolve to suffer alone.

## Keep a Journal

As we stated earlier, as soon as you realize that you might be getting a divorce from someone with BP, NP, or ASP traits, start keeping organized notes of incidents, parenting problems, violent episodes, rages, financial mismanagement, and so forth. Write down dates, times, what occurred, who else was present, and what action you took, if any. Note whether law enforcement, medical, or other professionals were involved, and keep copies of reports, case numbers, or both. Save email and text-message correspondence in a safe place, especially copies of hostile, harassing, and controversial exchanges.

## Copy Records

As soon as possible, quietly copy important documents: joint and separate bank account statements, your spouse's pay stubs, tax records, lists of assets and debts, and so forth. You never know if or when your partner may destroy important documents.

Keep in mind that the laws today require both parties to preserve their electronically stored information (ESI), so don't destroy any of yours. But it may be helpful to try to find your partner's ESI. Ask a lawyer how to request or subpoena this type of information.

## Prepare to Be Evicted

If you're still living in the same home, you might be forced to leave on very short notice because of an "emergency" court order kicking you out for alleged abuses. You may never get back into the house again. The court may allow your spouse to pack up your remaining belongings for you. We know of this happening in too many cases to count.

When blamers are involved, many valuable items and records may be damaged or disappear. Therefore, be prepared well in advance, if you can. Quietly move any valuables to a safe location and set aside funds for an emergency without taking more than your share, which you should discuss first with your attorney. Take pictures of your furniture and other valuable objects, and store these photos in a safe place.

*Thomas sought a therapist months before his case hit the courts, in an effort to learn how to handle Tammy's borderline mood swings and anger. Before he told Tammy he wanted a divorce, he retained an attorney who was familiar with difficult personalities and how the local court handled high-conflict cases. Thomas authorized the therapist and attorney to discuss the case with each other so that he could be well prepared for a potential battle.*

*Tammy had made abuse allegations against Thomas before. She had been violent with him and treated him as her target of blame for everything that was going wrong in her life. In anticipation of an escalating court dispute, he took out a loan from his retirement plan and told his employer he might need time off for a court battle. He received long-distance support from his siblings and prepared for whatever Tammy might do.*

*When Tammy made allegations that he had sexually abused their daughter, he was already very well prepared for the entire process. He knew that anger and false allegations would be her response to his request for a divorce, even though he did not know in advance which types of allegations she would make—and he was right.*

The more prepared you are for a court battle, the shorter and less disruptive it may be.

## Prepare for the Risk of Violence

There is always an increased risk of violence when someone leaves a relationship with a blamer. Even if there was no history of domestic violence in the past, many professionals are familiar with separation-instigated violence, as described in chapter 7. The blamer may feel extremely threatened, abandoned, or belittled. You should have a plan in place, especially before you leave a known physically abusive partner with BP, NP, or ASP traits. Your partner's exaggerated fears and anger may completely take over her behavior.

You should have a plan for protecting yourself and your children: a safe place to stay, money to live on, and people to assist you. Many books are available for you to educate yourself regarding domestic violence. Randi's booklet *Love and Loathing: Protecting Your Mental Health and Legal Rights When Your Partner Has Borderline Personality Disorder* (Eggshells Press, 2000) has a chapter on this subject. The national Domestic Violence Hotline is 800-799-7233.

## Shelters and Other Housing

There are more services and agencies now than ever before to provide assistance primarily for abused women. There are fewer services for abused men. The courts generally have hand-outs with contact information for domestic violence services, and the phone book may have lists of resources in your area where you and your children can stay for a few days and get services. The addresses are usually not public, so there may just be a phone number. If you have concerns about violence, strongly consider having a support person with you in court and having a plan for how to leave the building safely after difficult hearings. The courts today are generally supportive of this.

## Restraining Orders

Restraining orders may be helpful in setting limits on a blamer, but they are not guaranteed to protect you. In some cases, a restraining order may aggravate someone with severe BP, NP, or ASP traits, without providing strong protection. In a tragedy in Bill's community, a father killed his fourteen-year-old son on the street, right after a temporary restraining order was obtained against him. It was several years after the parents separated, but there had been ongoing custody and visitation disputes. He had threatened to kill his son, and the boy had told his therapist. His mother, with whom the son primarily lived, had apparently obtained the order.

Unfortunately, the father had a history of intense overat-tachment to his child (common to people with BP traits) and was preoccupied with how great he was at helping his son academically (common to people with NP traits). The week before he shot his son, the father had written a letter to the editor of a local newspaper, stating how his son's school and other parents should follow his example of tutoring his son two hundred hours in math over the prior year.

The "no contact" restraining order may have triggered such feelings of abandonment and narcissistic injury that it put the father over the edge, prompting him to kill his son—and then himself.

Not enough is known to be certain what caused this tragedy, and perhaps it would have occurred even if there had not been a restraining order. In either case, the boy's mother has lobbied hard for new laws requiring notice to the protected parties when restraining orders are to be served, so that there's time to get to a safe place while the person served with the order calms down. Check your state's laws about how such restraining orders work—and their limitations.

Violence is a potential real danger whenever a partner with BP, NP, or ASP traits is involved—even when there's no history of violence—because of the person's patterns of extreme thinking and emotions and vengeful behavior. Make sure to get information, support, and professional assistance in making your decisions and safety plans.

## Conclusion

Preparation is the key to managing your own separation and divorce. Prepare yourself emotionally for a bumpy road ahead, ideally with the help of a mental health professional. Prepare yourself financially, so that you can spring into action and have an attorney ready to do so as well on short notice. Make contacts with experts and be prepared to hire them to help you defend against possible blamer attacks. Prepare your family and friends to give you needed attention and emotional support from time to time.

Next, part 2 explains a lot about the issues involved when you face court litigation with a blamer who has BP, NP, or ASP traits. Part 2 will help you hire a lawyer (or at least consult one), learn about legal standards, and learn about how to handle potential problems if you do end up in court at any time.

Remember KEEP CALM: Now you have knowledge of blamer patterns of behavior and the energy to use this knowledge. You are in a good position to learn how to explain patterns of your blamer's behavior to legal professionals, as described throughout part 2, which focuses on the family court process. Then, part 3 focuses on the out-of-court issues of considering alternatives to litigation and managing your postdivorce relationship.

PART 2

# Succeeding in Family Court

Chapter 6

# Today's Divorce Court Culture

*Sarah realized that court was not at all what she had expected. "He just lied and got away with it," she exclaimed to her cousin. "It was over so quickly I didn't have time to organize my thoughts. I thought the judge would realize what was going on. I'm the mom, and our son should stay with me. Don't most moms get custody? Do you think I need to get an attorney?"*

Most people have never been to court. If you've seen court on television, in the movies, or in the news, you're not getting an accurate picture of today's family courts. In fact, high-profile trials often mislead the expectations of ordinary people who go to court, because those cases are primarily criminal cases with a lot of resources on both sides to investigate and present information.

In reality, most family court trials or hearings are relatively short; you rarely get your "day in court." The issues are very limited, and what you really want to say is often considered irrelevant. The outcome is rarely satisfying—even if you win—and court orders are often unenforceable when applied to someone with BP, NP, or ASP traits because of the person's psychological inability to accept them. Once these people get to family court, they are blamers all the way, and their volatile emotions just escalate after each hearing rather than calm down. These people often can't stop themselves when they win (it encourages them) or when they lose (it enrages them).

You will be less surprised and more successful if you're prepared for these predictable problems in court:

- The blamer's anger and allegations are given much more credibility at the beginning of the case than you expect.

- Some decisions are made very quickly at first ("emergencies" requiring restraining orders, supervised visitation with children, control of funds, and so on). Then a long, drawn-out process of very slow information gathering and decision making at subsequent hearings or trials may follow, often spanning several months or years. Or there may be no further information gathering, and the quick decisions will stick, whether or not they are based on accurate information.

- Hearings are brief, arguments are highly emotional, facts are in dispute and hard to verify, and assumptions are often made. "He said, she said" declarations often cancel each other out; the facts of interpersonal conflict are usually unverifiable, because only the people who were present know what has occurred, and much of the most accurate information is excluded by legal objections, such as "hearsay" (statements heard and passed on by others, which are considered automatically unreliable).

- The process costs much more money than you ever expect.

- The final divorce orders are less favorable, less specific, and less enforceable than you expect.

Given the common concerns of targets and the importance of knowing how to handle your court case, it is essential to know what today's family court is like and how to deal with it. We think of it as the family court "culture," because it's about more than just procedures; it's also about the predictable ways everyone thinks and acts in today's family court.

# Family Court Is Highly Adversarial

In most states you have a choice about whether to get divorced by agreement or by a judge deciding on the issues. In many cases, you don't have to go to court at all to get divorced. We estimate that about 80 percent of couples untie the knot without any significant court involvement. Their agreements are based on fifty years of "no-fault" divorce laws, which have established rules and guidelines for everything from basic parenting schedules to child support to dividing pensions.

This means that people who go to court are in conflict over something other than the basic rules. While occasionally the issue is some new policy that needs the court to set a precedent, the usual disputes are about personality-based disagreements. When blamers are involved, the case usually becomes about the basic facts, not the law. Because of their constant distortions and the intense emotions that go with them, facts are highly in dispute and become a bitter battle, as the blamer desperately promotes and defends her distorted point of view.

Since interpersonal conflict is one of the diagnostic criteria for the diagnosis of a personality disorder, it's not surprising that many of the divorces involving people with these PDs or their traits dominate family court calendars and escalate into highly adversarial cases. For most reasonable people, the structure of the court acts as a calming and limit-setting process, because disputes are resolved when the judge makes a decision. Unfortunately, the court process tends to escalate disputes for those with personality problems because of their lack of coping skills and inability to accept and heal from loss. When they "win," it's often based on such distortions of information that reasonable people are compelled to seek a revised decision.

The court is an adversarial system. Decisions are based on a "win-lose" structure. Theoretically, the adversarial system levels the playing field and allows both the accuser and the accused the opportunity to be heard and to be patiently understood before a decision is made. In reality, many of this system's good intentions backfire when the adversarial thinking and behavior of a blamer is involved.

When it comes to interpersonal disputes, the adversarial system benefits people who are more aggressive and more effective at blaming others and who can present a case in simple terms. As people involved with blamers know, these are characteristics blamers possess more than the average reasonable person. Therefore, to the surprise of many people, blamers are often successful in court—at least at the beginning and sometimes throughout the entire case—because their adversarial thinking fits so well with the court's adversarial approach to decision making, as shown in this chart about the blaming characteristics of high-conflict people.

## Similar Characteristics of High-Conflict People and Court

| Characteristics of High-Conflict People | Characteristics of Court Process |
|---|---|
| Lifetime preoccupation is blaming others. | Purpose is deciding whom to blame, who's "guilty." |
| Avoid taking responsibility. | The court will hold someone else responsible. |
| Engage in all-or-nothing thinking. | "Guilty" and "not guilty" are usually the only choices. |
| Always seek attention and sympathy. | They can be the center of attention and sympathy. |
| Aggressively seek allies in their causes. | Can bring numerous advocates to court. |
| Speak in dramatic, emotional extremes. | Can argue, testify in dramatic, emotional extremes. |
| Focus intensely on others' past behavior. | Can hear, give testimony on others' past behavior. |
| Punish people who are guilty of "hurting" them. | Court is the place to impose maximum punishment. |
| Try to get others to solve their problems. | Get the court to solve their problems. |
| It's okay to lie if they feel desperate. | Lying (perjury) is rarely acknowledged or punished. |

The adversarial court process and the blaming, all-or-nothing way of thinking of high-conflict people (borderline and narcissistic blamers appear to be the most common such people in family courts) are a perfect fit. Yet court was never designed to be a way of life. It is a formal method for solving very specific disputes in an isolated, all-or-nothing way that doesn't work in daily life or in relationships.

Unfortunately, this adversarial way of thinking is the way of life for many blamers, which gives them a great advantage in court. Your ordinary problem-solving methods, which work best in daily life (cooperation, showing empathy, listening without interruption, softening criticism, and so on) may actually backfire in court. Blamers' desperate charm and aggressive drive may succeed at making them look innocent. Many cases that the court views as two high-conflict people fighting are actually driven by only one party who successfully makes the other party look bad.

**The parties can say anything.** Freedom of speech is one of the cornerstones of our free society. Unfortunately, this freedom encourages blamers to make false or reckless statements in court based on their cognitive distortions, without concern for their accuracy or consequences. There is rarely any penalty for perjury. Unfortunately, blamers may be greatly rewarded for aggressively making false statements: they may get more time with the children, have better support payments, and receive more of the property.

As a result, blamers tend to make dramatic statements from the start of the case and to escalate with more dramatic statements whenever they are confronted. As the target works hard to gather and present accurate information in response and to resolve the issues, the blamer often raises new allegations, which keeps the level of conflict escalated and unresolved.

**The parties can keep coming back.** Family courts are different from civil and criminal courts worldwide, in that some of the most difficult decisions can be continually brought back to court for rehearing. Parenting decisions and support decisions are usually "modifiable" with a change of circumstances. This means that at any time either party can allege a change of circumstances, initiate a full hearing in court, and force the other party to participate. The consequence for unnecessary relitigation is usually just a lecture from the judge, which has little effect on a blamer.

**The parties can make lots of demands.** Both parties have legal rights to demand documents, take depositions, subpoena witnesses, and schedule hearings at court. The other party has to comply, or else important decisions can be made against that person. Blamers take full advantage of this process, called "discovery." They may investigate, intrude, follow, and harass you and your supporters, all under the guise of exercising legal rights.

The result of all of these procedural rights is that blamers use their manipulative skills to the maximum. In contrast, targets tend to be respectful problem solvers, who avoid unnecessary confrontation, rudeness, and intrusion. This reality puts targets between a rock (just tolerating all of these highly adversarial behaviors without responding) and a hard place (responding and participating in a highly distasteful, adversarial manner). We will discuss how to handle this dilemma throughout part 2. The focus is on how to explain patterns of the blamer's unchanging harmful behavior and false statements to each of the professionals involved in family court (lawyers, evaluators, judges, mediators, and others).

# Get Over It?

Starting in 1970, most states adopted "no-fault" divorce laws to end the necessity for allegations of adultery, abandonment, spousal abuse, and so forth in obtaining a divorce. The parties were instructed to focus on parenting, support, and property decisions, rather than make negative, blaming remarks about each other. In the 1980s, court mediation programs were established to assist parents in making decisions about child custody and visitation (also known as "access"). Mental health professionals became an important part of the court process and further discouraged the parties from making blaming remarks.

In this family court culture, divorce has become treated as an intense and temporary conflict between ordinary, equal people who just need to be reminded to focus on the future, not the past: "Just get over it!" Thus, it's common for courts to try to reduce the conflict between the parties by simply telling both parties to stop criticizing each other. If one party says the other is lying, the judge often assumes both are lying. If one says the other has misbehaved, the court generally assumes that both have misbehaved and that these minor problems will end once the divorce is over.

When a party raises concerns about the personality of the other party, it's common for the courts to try to stop such comments, because they are considered unnecessarily disparaging. This makes it particularly difficult for people facing a borderline, narcissistic, or antisocial blamer. If you say that the person has a PD, the court may chastise you and view you as the one making inappropriate comments. Legal professionals often assume that if one partner has a PD, then both have a PD.

For this reason, we encourage you to explain patterns of behavior, rather than label the person's personality in court, as described in chapter 14.

# Abuse Allegations May Be Presumed True

A new layer of family court culture was added in the 1990s with the rise of society's concerns over substance abuse, child abuse, and spousal abuse (also known as domestic violence or intimate partner violence). Laws changed to provide increased protection for victims of abuse and consequences for abusers. These were very positive steps after years of denial of some crucial problems, because people with these behaviors often have a very hard time stopping themselves.

Many (perhaps most) of the people engaged in abusive behaviors in divorce cases have the characteristics of borderline, narcissistic, or antisocial personalities: they lack impulse control, are preoccupied with blaming others, and don't change their behavior even when it gets them into trouble. Some researchers have identified a borderline pattern of behavior as the most common among domestic-violence perpetrators, with their emotional cycle of built-up tension, an angry outburst, and a period of remorse (Dutton 2007). Other researchers describe many of the behaviors of narcissistic personalities when they explain batterer parents, with their self-centeredness and an attitude of ownership toward their spouses and children (Bancroft and Silverman 2002). And antisocial abusers are understood to be the ones who are more intentional or instrumental about their violence on the way to getting something they want or for punishing their partner for challenging their dominance over them.

The large federal study described in chapter 2 also indicates that people with BPD (Grant et al. 2008), NPD (Stinson et al. 2008), and ASPD (Grant et al. 2004) have a higher incidence of substance abuse than average, which may contribute to these impulsive, abusive behaviors.

People with BP, NP, or ASP traits repeat their problems over and over again, including abusive behaviors, and may not stop until they experience serious legal consequences. Courts, including criminal and family courts, have the potential for restraining their behavior and motivating them to get treatment through a combination of possible jail time and restricted access to their children. But this varies widely between court systems and individual judges, and often there are very limited consequences for abusive behavior.

Family courts today are faced with more allegations of abusive behavior than ever before, but with very little training and experience in recognizing these problems and the personalities that drive them. Many legal professionals (lawyers, counselors, evaluators, and judges) have presumptions about abuse, based on their own work and life experience. Many of them believe that false allegations are rare, so they immediately assume reports of abuse are true and focus instead on what the consequences should be. (Others assume that allegations made in family court are usually false and made to get an advantage, which we will address in the next section.)

It's important for you to know that the abuse allegations in the next chapter are frequently raised in family court and given immediate attention. You need to fully understand how the court looks at each of these issues.

If you have been abusive in any of these ways, it's better to admit it right away and show how you're getting treatment so that it won't happen again. If you have not been abusive, then you need to have information ready to help explain the facts. Otherwise, you will be caught by surprise, as Sarah was, when any of the issues in chapter 7 are raised.

# Abuse Allegations May Be Presumed False

Unfortunately, people with BP, NP, or ASP traits also make a lot of false allegations throughout their lives because of their cognitive distortions (all-or-nothing thinking, emotional reasoning, jumping to conclusions, and so on) and their emotional hurt, anger, shame, and defensiveness. They generally see themselves as victims of abuse, since they can't see their own part in their life problems. With these dynamics, it's not surprising that people with BP, NP, or ASP traits make a lot of false allegations in court against people they used to love.

Some judges and other professionals have swung in the opposite direction from presumptions of abuse and assume that allegations of abuse are probably false. Be prepared for the possibility that you will be accused of making false allegations when you present the court with accurate information about the blamer's violence, child abuse, or other abusive behaviors. It may help to find out if your county's family court or your specific judge seems to have any unconscious presumptions about abuse or false allegations.

# Decisions May Be Made Very Quickly or Very Slowly

In many family court cases, important decisions are made at emergency hearings before the case has really begun. Then, the impression the judge receives sticks in her mind throughout the case. The judge may quickly make decisions unfavorable to you, and then the process of investigation to determine whether such rulings should be modified may be slow. There are four basic types of court events for decisions in separation and divorce cases, and predictable problems can occur in each one: emergency ("ex parte") hearings, regular hearings, trials, and postdivorce hearings. (However, none of these are normally required if your case settles out of court.)

## Emergency Hearings

In some jurisdictions, emergency hearings are called ex parte hearings. They are for emergency orders, such as temporary restraining or protective orders (TROs), emergency child custody or visitation orders (because of alleged abuse or possible flight risk), or freezing of funds or bank accounts. An emergency ex parte hearing may be the way your case begins, often with only one party present. Ex parte hearings occur with short notice or no notice to the other party, if it's alleged that the other party would become dangerous. They can be necessary and helpful in protecting a party or child from abuse, such as from a raging blamer, but they can also be misused by a party making false allegations. They can create a status quo that's hard to overcome.

In Thomas's case, an evaluation was ordered with a hearing in three months. It's not uncommon for these evaluations to take longer, and hearings on huge issues such as child sexual abuse are commonly continued (postponed) a couple of times before everyone is ready. Evaluations commonly go six to twelve months in cases like these. But for now, Thomas thinks it will be resolved in three months, so he feels patient and hopeful and isn't taking much action. He is relying on everything going well in the long run. He is mistaken.

## Regular Hearings

Regular hearings are often called "order to show cause" (OSC) hearings, "request for orders" (RFO) hearings, or some other name, depending on your jurisdiction. These are the most frequent types of hearings for family court decisions, which usually last about twenty to forty minutes and focus on narrow issues, often for temporary orders about child support, alimony, custody, and visitation. Most of these issues are modifiable and expected to be addressed again at a later hearing with more extensive information.

These hearings focus on declarations or brief court testimony, depending on your local court's rules. There are local rules and deadlines for how the parties and attorneys need to prepare for these hearings. The judge needs to be adequately informed to make temporary decisions that may last for weeks or even years. If you represent yourself, the judge will expect you to present your case with the same basic level of knowledge of the law and procedures as an attorney. We generally recommend against representing yourself when dealing with a blamer. If nothing else, have a consultation with a family law attorney before deciding whether to represent yourself. When someone with BP, NP, or ASP traits is involved, you generally need an attorney to help you quickly manage all of the unpredictable and impulsive legal maneuvers that may occur in your case. It may take you too long on your own to figure out how to respond legally to a blamer's surprise attacks and it may be hard to reverse the damage later on.

Likewise, blamers desperately want to be in control of the legal process and often drag out the divorce to avoid feeling abandoned, losing self-esteem, or losing their power and control over you. Therefore, it helps to have an attorney who knows the rules and procedures about what steps the other party can legally delay and how to require court action.

## Trials

Trials are much less common in family courts than emergency hearings and regular hearings, because they take so much of the judge's time. The judges have so many cases that trials are often scheduled for six to twelve months later. Therefore, it's common for parties to adopt the temporary orders made at hearings as their permanent divorce orders. Most parties just settle their cases out of court with the help of attorneys or a mediator, but if they don't settle, many courts require them to attend settlement conferences at court weeks before the trial can occur.

Trials often include property-division issues, long-term alimony decisions, child support, and long-term custody and visitation orders. But when people with BP, NP, or ASP traits are involved, trials are often about abuse, false allegations, or an unwillingness to accept the legal standards on an issue. From Bill's experience, most family court trials today involve someone with BP, NP, or ASP traits, because everyone else is flexible enough and cost-conscious enough to find ways to resolve their issues out of court based on existing standards.

## Postdivorce Hearings

You may be surprised to know that additional hearings often occur in cases with people with BP, NP, or ASP traits, even after the divorce decision or major custody decisions have been made. Perhaps a month or a year later, blamers may bring a matter back to court for a modification because they never liked the decision in the first place, they act out in a manner that requires them to be brought back to court by the other party, or there's a legitimate issue that remains to be resolved.

At most postdivorce hearings, the party who wants to modify the prior orders must prove a "change of circumstances." In many cases involving people with BP, NP, or ASP traits, the change is their own escalating behavior, or nothing has changed and they just don't like the prior decisions.

Blamers are notorious for not accepting court orders. Acceptance is part of the grieving process, and people with PDs have a difficult time grieving. Years ago, Elisabeth Kübler-Ross (1969) identified the five stages of the grieving process. Blamers seem to be stuck in the anger phase (striking out at others) or depression phase (making suicide attempts or frequently crying years after the divorce as though it were yesterday) without ever reaching acceptance.

Overall, the pace of your case is very likely to be fast at the outset and then very slow. The main reason for delays in cases with blamers is that the allegations they make may appear credible to the court and therefore require extensive evaluations and numerous hearings. There's often little clear-cut information but such strong emotions that the court is concerned that abuse may be happening that is not, or that it's just strong emotions when something abusive really is occurring. Blamers can be highly persuasive with their strong emotions.

The chart in the next section helps explain how some cases start out so badly in family court and why it's essential to get problem-solving professionals and objective evaluators in the case as quickly as possible.

# Emotional Persuasion Heavily Influences Family Court

In court, the goal is to make a decision. Once a decision is made, the issue is resolved and the court moves on. Decisions are based on the adversaries' persuasiveness. The most persuasive party (or the person's attorney) will prevail, and the least persuasive party will lose. Theoretically, this encourages the production of facts and arguments with which the court will determine the best policy for handling the problem at hand. In reality, the most persuasive party is often the one who prevails with peripheral persuasion: persuasion that goes on outside conscious attention.

Peripheral persuasion is a concept that has been studied for decades by those involved with advertising, politics, and negotiations (Lewicki, Barry, and Saunders 2010). Its indirect methods match the emotional persuasion of blamers with BP, NP, or ASP traits in court:

- Attractiveness of the messenger

- Aggressiveness of the messenger

- Confidence displayed

- More arguments made

- Intensity of language

- Shorter sentences and simpler ideas

- Use of distractions

- Emotional appeal

Recent brain research indicates that the person with the most emotional facial expressions will dominate a group in the absence of a hierarchy (Goleman 2006). That easily describes people with BP, NP, or ASP traits, who are repeatedly expressing their charm, anger, tears, and intense expressions of fear. This is all highly contagious—and mostly unconscious. It influences family, friends, and professionals. Compare the following two charts on contributing roles in high-conflict divorce to see how this process works.

## Emotional Persuasion: How Negative Advocates Absorb and Escalate Conflict

| | |
|---|---|
| Common Cognitive Distortions in Blamers: ⇩ | *I'm so upset. I feel like a victim, so I must be a victim.* <br><br> *The other party made me feel this way. It's all that person's fault.* <br><br> *I'm not responsible for the problem or the solution.* |
| Emotional Response in Friends and Family: ⇩ | *You're so upset; someone must have hurt you and your child.* <br><br> *You should sue the jerk.* <br><br> *We'll help you go to court.* |
| Emotional Response in Counselors and Other Helping Professionals: ⇩ | *You are so upset; I couldn't possibly challenge you.* <br><br> *I believe everything you're telling me.* |
| Emotional Response in Attorneys: ⇩ | *You are so upset; I will fight for you. I will argue that whatever you told me is true.* |
| Emotional Response in Judges: | *Your information is upsetting. Harm must be happening. Your story feels more credible to me than the other party's. Just to be safe, I will make orders against the other party.* |

## Fact Finding: How Problem Solvers Analyze and Resolve Conflict

| | |
|---|---|
| Judges: ⇩ | *I'll never know what really happened. I will make temporary orders and no assumptions. Just to be safe, I will order an evaluation.* |
| Objective, Trained Evaluators: ⇩ | *I will consider any and all information you can provide. I will look at many sources of information with an open mind. I will recommend solutions, rather than blame.* |
| Attorneys: ⇩ | *I will vigorously defend you against false attacks, but I won't argue what I don't know or believe. Let's carefully uncover the facts together.* |
| Counselors and Other Helping Professionals: ⇩ | *Let's look at your part in this matter, however small. Choose your battles. Focus on your goals, not reacting. Let's look at what you can do to help yourself and your child.* |
| Friends and Family: ⇩ | *We can support you without taking sides. We can provide resources and helpful information. We will listen and help you think of solutions.* |
| You, Examining Your Own Cognitive Distortions: | *I know I'm upset, which affects my thinking right now. I'll get advice before drawing conclusions or making decisions. I'll provide information, look at my own part, and look for solutions.* |

The first chart shows how persuasive blamers can prevail in court. Their heightened emotions, "emotional facts," and simple tales of being victimized by those close to them are peripherally persuasive. This persuasion is generally unconscious to the listener and therefore more powerful. Thus, the decision-making process in family court often favors them.

Only a very aware person or professional can resist this peripheral emotional persuasion. The first chart shows how emotional persuasion can escalate a case. It most often occurs at the beginning of a case, with false allegations of abuse or emotional denials of true abuse. It may or may not get turned around over the course of the case. The first chart shows a time line of escalation, and the second shows de-escalation and problem solving in some cases. In other cases, all the decisions are made based on emotional persuasion, and fact finding never seriously occurs.

Given the lack of time for most decisions, minds are quickly made up, urgent action is taken (or not taken), new information is unconsciously ruled out, and biases against targets are hard to undo. With this in mind, it's often essential to bring an objective, trained evaluator into the case to get under the surface of emotional persuasion.

## Evaluators Are Very Important

Though evaluators are not a required part of the family court process, they are often the most important decision makers in high-conflict family court cases today. They are appointed by the court to investigate and analyze the case and then make recommendations to the court.

Evaluators have more time to get to know the parties (their public and private personas) and more expertise, such as a psychologist who can do psychological testing or a CPA who can analyze financial reports. This is the reason why courts rely so heavily on their recommendations. In the vast majority of cases, the courts adopt their recommendations with only minor changes, but some courts prefer not to use evaluators very often, so you may need to lobby hard for an evaluation if—especially if—your spouse has been a very persuasive blamer.

Choosing the evaluator and providing information to that person are two of the most important aspects of your case. During the evaluation process, you will generally meet with the evaluator without your attorney present. Therefore, being adequately prepared, knowing what's important to communicate, and developing a friendly bond with the evaluator will be essential. Preparing for your evaluation is discussed in depth in chapter 11, which focuses on many issues related to evaluators.

## The Burden Is on You

Because family courts are based on the adversarial system of law, each party bears the burden of obtaining, submitting, and arguing evidence. Rather than give the judge the responsibility to investigate the underlying facts, the parties are responsible for obtaining evidence and presenting it to the court. The judge's role is to decide which facts and arguments will prevail.

Thus, the burden is not on the judge or the evaluator (to whom you provide evidence), but on you to come up with the relevant evidence and to present it in an easy-to-digest and persuasive manner. Because you bear the burden, it's imperative that you speak with an attorney for a proper assessment of your case. The decision to represent yourself carries great risks.

Sarah discovered this from her first ex parte hearing and was advised to get an attorney. She will need to work hard to rehabilitate her image in the eyes of the court. In his case, Thomas already had an attorney, but he still has a lot of work to do.

# Conclusion

Today's family court culture has three dominant and conflicting trends among professionals: they believe both parties are equal contributors to any conflicts; they quickly believe the first person who says abuse has occurred; or they quickly disregard allegations of abuse, including those that may be true. The emotional persuasion of people with BP, NP, or ASP traits plays right into these unconscious presumptions, so that they often prevail, especially at the beginning of a case, unless you are very well prepared.

In the long run, facts can prevail in family court so that an honest person who accurately portrays facts can be successful. The next few chapters will tell you how you can succeed within this court culture. Your attorney will know what the procedures are but is less likely to know the dynamics of borderline, narcissistic, and antisocial personalities. The burden will be on you to find an attorney you can work with and share your knowledge about these dynamics. Chapters 8 and 9 address these issues. If possible, do not try to handle the burdens of family court alone.

# Chapter 7

# Abuse, Alienation, and False Allegations

The following issues are a major focus of family court hearings and can influence decisions about protective orders, parenting time, child support, spousal support, who gets to stay in the house, and other seemingly unrelated decisions. In many cases, the judge makes good decisions that are protective of the children and survivors of abuse and may actually lead to improvements in behavior. In other cases, the judge may be misled and misunderstands the true dynamics of the case. People with BP, NP, and ASP personalities are particularly driven to raise these issues or defend their prior behavior in a manner that causes injustice to be done. Being prepared to explain the true nature of these issues may make a big difference in your case. The following explanations may help you understand these problems and explain them to decision makers.

## Substance Abuse

Allegations of substance abuse are one of the most common complaints raised in family court, especially in regard to parenting ability. Someone with a drug or alcohol addiction can be ordered to have supervised visitation and required to attend a treatment program. When the person makes enough progress, he can come back to court to have these requirements lifted. This has been a very effective area for the courts, motivating many parents to deal with these real problems.

## False Allegations of Substance Abuse

Unfortunately, many blamers with substance-abuse problems defend themselves by projecting their behavior onto the target and falsely accusing that person of substance abuse. While sometimes both parties have a substance-abuse problem, in many cases only the blamer does. Fortunately, drug testing and assessments can usually show who has the problem. While the courts are limited in their use of these methods, they have become fairly accurate in identifying and addressing these problems.

*In Sarah's case, her husband successfully convinced the judge to believe that she was a parent with a substance-abuse problem, although it was not true. It was true that she took medication and that she overslept one day. On the surface, these could be symptoms of a pill addiction, and the court appears to have adopted that concern. But if someone were to go to her house and observe her daily behavior, she would not fit the description Sam gave to the court of a depressed and neglectful pill addict. While all of these allegations raise concerns, they are a combination of exaggerations and knowingly false statements by her husband. It will take an accurate substance-abuse assessment, which the court has ordered, to determine whether these allegations of substance abuse are true.*

*Sam is actually projecting his own use of substances onto Sarah. He has an alcohol problem and often had been drinking when he hit her, but, not wanting to embarrass him, she did not bring up this issue in court. As a result, no substance-abuse assessment was ordered for Sam.*

# Child Abuse

There are generally four types of child abuse described in state laws: physical abuse, neglect, sexual abuse, and emotional abuse. It is important to note that in some states spanking with an object (belt, paddle, wooden spoon) is considered physical abuse, while in others such spanking is more tolerated. Physical abuse and neglect are often successfully treated in parenting-skills training programs.

Child sexual abuse is extremely hard to treat, and it may not be considered treatable at all, depending on your court. This is a very troubling area that often involves a narcissistic or antisocial personality disorder. Such abusers often seriously lack empathy or remorse for their behavior. Some were sexually abused themselves as children, but others have no history of child sexual abuse and it may be more related to a drive to completely dominate and control another person.

Emotional abuse is allowed to be reported as child abuse in some states but generally is not given much weight in family court decisions, since it is alleged in so many divorce cases and considered very difficult to evaluate.

When child abuse is alleged against a parent, family courts often limit that parent's time with the child, require supervised visitation, or impose a temporary "no contact" order (sometimes used when a sexual-abuse allegation is being investigated). These are powerful court orders designed to protect children. Frequently, the abusive parent is someone with borderline traits, who alternately clings to the children and then rages at them when she feels threatened, or a narcissist who sees himself as owning the children and free to do whatever he wants with them. Those with antisocial traits range from viciously abusing a child, physically or sexually, to teaching the child antisocial behaviors, to having little interest in the child at all.

## False Allegations of Child Abuse

The courts take allegations of abuse very seriously and many judges see child protection and protecting victims of domestic violence as their biggest responsibilities. But some blamers make false allegations of child abuse, either knowingly to get an advantage, or unconsciously because of their own sincere beliefs about the other parent. Such allegations can give them a great deal of power in court over issues of custody and visitation or access, because these activate the judge's concern about protecting vulnerable people. The target can almost be eliminated as a parent if strong enough allegations are made and the court accepts them as true.

> As Thomas experienced, the courts often treat child-abuse allegations very seriously. The judge said, "Just to be safe, I am ordering supervised visitation. This order is without prejudice to either party, which means I am making no assumptions about whether the allegations are true or not, and today's order will have no weight in my final decision. Just to be safe, the child will be in the temporary sole legal and physical custody of the mother."
>
> In reality, the child would be safer in Thomas's care, but the judge does not know that yet. There is often an unwritten presumption of truth in abuse allegations, and the judge does not want to be the one with her picture in the newspaper for allowing a child to be sexually abused. The rationale is that if it turns out to be false, the child was safe anyway. Of course, this abuse presumption does not recognize that the "safe" mother has BPD and emotionally abuses the child on a regular basis.

# Domestic Violence

In the mid-1990s, state and federal lawmakers passed many bills requiring family courts to generate findings, treatment orders, and restraining orders regarding the abuse of one spouse by the other. In 2008, family-law and domestic-violence experts held a conference to increase understanding and effectiveness in dealing with this serious problem. They concluded that there are actually four distinctly different types of domestic violence (Kelly and Johnson 2008) or Intimate Partner Violence (IPV) as it is sometimes called.

1.  **Coercive controlling violence.** Also known as batter-ing, this behavior involves a pattern of power and control by one partner and a pattern of fear in the victim (also known as the survivor). There may not be frequent vio-lence, but when violence occurs, it can be severe and result in bruises, broken bones, and even death. The victim often becomes isolated, loses self-esteem, and finds it very hard to leave. Batterers are primarily male, although perhaps 15 percent are female, with the same dynamics against their male partners. Most batterers seem to have characteristics of borderline, narcissistic, or antisocial personality disorders.

    Courts commonly order batterer's treatment groups for batterers, which may last twelve, twenty-six, or fifty-two weeks, depending on your court system. These pro-grams are generally helpful for batterers with borderline or impulsive narcissistic traits, because they learn how to prevent the buildup of anger and how to challenge the cognitive distortions that lead them to blame their spouses and justify violence. Batterers who have antiso-cial or controlled narcissistic traits are less affected by these treatment programs, because they don't see them-selves as having an "anger management" problem; they are able to manage their anger very well to achieve their own controlling purposes.

2.  **Situational couple violence.** This type of domestic violence is the most common type. Instead of a pattern of power and control, both parties in the couple have difficulties resolving conflict peacefully and get into pushing and shoving types of behavior, sometimes with injuries. Neither party lives in fear of the other, and the violence is generally less severe. Research shows that men and women engage in this type of violence fairly equally and that they are less likely to have PDs than batterers.

3.  **Separation-instigated violence.** Sometimes there are one or two incidents at the time of separation, but no prior history of violence. Both parties may engage in this behavior, and it is fairly equal among males and females.

4.  **Violent resistance.** *Violent resistance* is the term used when a victim or survivor of a batterer fights back, sometimes injuring the usual perpetrator. Sometimes, batterers set up a spouse to fight back, then call the police. Sometimes victims get arrested because of one injury to the batterer, while the batterer gets away with numerous injuries on other occasions that the victim does not report. Sometimes survivors who fight back are more severely injured, so this is not a recommended solution.

Unfortunately, while many counselors are aware of these four types of domestic violence, many lawyers and judges are not. Some have presumptions that any incident of domestic violence is always a sign of a batterer, and they treat it very severely. Others have presumptions that minimize domestic violence, and they assume it will stop on its own. Both unofficial presumptions can be terribly wrong, but in the adversarial process, with huge caseloads and little training, judges have to make on-the-spot decisions, and unofficial presumptions exist, whether they are recognized or not.

The best situation is for all the professionals involved to be well informed and open-minded. This is rarely the case in the adversarial process of family court, as so much time is spent arguing over presumptions when there are very few facts. That is why you will need to be well prepared with detailed information for explaining the true behavior pattern that truly needs restraining, or responding to allegations of abuse against you, even though there may be no basis for them. Having a restraining order granted or denied is often quite uncertain, so get good advice and be prepared for it to go either way.

## False Allegations of Domestic Violence

Some training materials for court professionals have said that women don't lie when they accuse men of domestic violence. While this is generally true, many professionals have told us that they have dealt with examples of women (often with BPD or ASPD) who do lie about domestic violence, either for revenge or because of their cognitive distortions.

Some men (generally with antisocial traits) lie about their wives, claiming that they abuse their children or husbands. People with antisocial personalities are the most persuasive blamers of all, because they have been lying all their lives and lack remorse. Not surprisingly, the same person making false allegations against the other parent may actually be abusing that parent as well.

Sometimes, if you're falsely accused of domestic violence and you start convincing the court of this, the blamer will claim that you're very clever and manipulative and always get away with it. In other words, they may say there is no evidence because you have the characteristics of batterers with antisocial traits, who often escape detection. This is why the facts and how you present them are so important.

Some male victims of domestic violence have been accused by their wives of being violent and of cleverly conning their therapists, their doctors, their attorneys, and the courts. This becomes very confusing for the courts, because they have traditionally believed women more than men on this subject. Nevertheless, this may be changing. Many courts are now more skeptical and realize that some women (and some men) lie about abuse and that sometimes the woman is the abusive party.

Domestic violence is a top concern of some lawyers, therapists, and family court judges. They may have strong feelings that blamers can easily manipulate, or they may be very knowledgeable and hard to mislead. Try to find out who you are dealing with in advance.

# Legal Impact of Findings of Abuse

Depending on state laws, people who are found guilty of domestic violence or child abuse may be kicked out of their houses without notice, denied the right to have custody for several years, given only supervised visitation, made to pay higher spousal support, and given restraining orders to stay away from their spouses.

In terms of overall credibility, someone accused of abuse could be negatively stereotyped throughout the court case. This can affect a wide variety of discretionary decisions that may be unrelated to any abuse, such as calculating monthly child or spousal support when income figures are disputed, dividing up accounts when their values are disputed, and determining whether a parent gets to move out of state with a minor child.

*Credibility is everything in family court.* Someone accused of abuse may instantly lose sympathy and credibility in the eyes of the court. Only a rapid, fact-based response can prevent a negative stereotype from attaching to you if you're falsely accused of abuse. Likewise, someone making an emotional request for protective orders may be seen as exaggerating and overly emotional, so that a negative stereotype attaches to you. Ideally, you need to be prepared to appear calm and reasonable, with a fact-based response from the start of the case.

# Parental Alienation

*Parental alienation* is a controversial term for a child's resistance or refusal to spend time with one of the parents during and after a separation and divorce (the rejected parent), while totally agreeing with the other parent (the favored parent). Most therapists, attorneys, and judges believe this occurs, but there is intense disagreement over what has "caused" this problem. Some parents and professionals believe it is because one parent has purposely alienated the child from the other. Many call this "parental alienation syndrome" (PAS), although most mental health professionals and legal professionals have not generally recognized such a syndrome, and it is not listed in the *DSM-5* as a mental disorder.

Other parents and professionals believe that this resistance is caused by the rejected parent's own behavior. They believe that the child is "realistically estranged" from that parent because of abusive behavior or extremely bad parenting skills (Johnston, Roseby, and Kuehnle 2009). Many high-conflict family court cases are about determining whether a child who resists contact with a parent was abused by that parent or alienated by the other parent. While most professionals believe "alienation" exists in some form, many believe it is caused by more than one factor.

Bill has analyzed this subject in depth, the results of which are in his book *Don't Alienate the Kids! Raising Resilient Children While Avoiding High Conflict Divorce*, 2nd edition (Unhooked Books, 2020). This book contains many suggestions for how to deal with this problem, including family counseling or skills training, such as his New Ways for Families® counseling or online program.

It appears that alienation occurs mostly unconsciously when a child is repeatedly exposed to one parent's all-or-nothing thinking, unmanaged emotions, and extreme behaviors, which is typical of parents with PDs. However, these extremes may unintentionally be reinforced by the other parent by getting angry at the child about their resistance, or being passive in the face of the blamer's behavior, or actually accepting the child's rejection and ending contact with the child. Other family members play a role, as well as family law professionals and the larger "culture of blame" we live in today (Eddy 2020).

The negative stereotyping of the target appears to lead the child to generate negative "emotional facts" about being treated poorly or seriously abused by the target. These exaggerated or false "facts" often add to the blamer's fears about the other parent and become a focus of concern and investigation in court. Even though they are primarily influenced unconsciously, such children can essentially become negative advocates for the blamer as the favored parent.

Avoid getting angry at the child, as it's not their fault. Sometimes a child says: "Please don't contact me anymore. I never want to see you again." Sometimes a parent says: "Okay, then I'll stop having any contact with you." This is understandable but undesirable. Instead, it's better to say, "I understand you are caught in the middle, but such all-or-nothing thinking is not healthy for you. You need two parents to learn from to have a successful life. If you do this, I will still love you and I'll send cards from time to time with my tips for a good life."

Then send notes with tips that you have learned, so that you are not directly discussing the child's current actions, but focusing on her future life. The benefit of this approach is that when your child eventually recontacts you (which most do months or years later), she may blame you for not caring (yes, this is ironic but true). This way you can show how you cared. Therefore, save copies of any cards and notes you send.

## False Allegations of Alienation

Now that alienation is becoming more widespread and is occurring against both mothers and fathers as the rejected parent, some blamers are accusing their targets of alienating the children. As with other forms of abuse, blamers can make false allegations of alienation against you. Since alienation grabs the court's attention, some blamers have gained a lot of power and control over the children by convincing the court that you are alienating the children.

The best way to avoid decisions against you for this reason is to tell the children you support their relationship with the other parent, to make sure not to interfere with that parent's scheduled time, to avoid exposing the children to angry phone calls and negative comments, and to make positive comments about the other parent from time to time. It also may be necessary to seek a psychological evaluation to show to the decision makers that you are not engaging in alienating behavior.

## Relocation Issues

Relocation (or "move-away") is the term that courts often use when one parent wants to move with the children to another county, state, or country. These can be very difficult cases because it's obvious that it will impact the children's time and relationship with one of the parents. It's just a question of how much it will impact them.

Not surprisingly, relocation often arises when there is a BP, NP, or ASP involved in a family court case. It may be that you will feel the need to get away from him by moving far, far away.

Yet the courts do not support that approach for that purpose. It may be that the BP, NP, or ASP wants to cut you off from your child by pursuing such a move. Remember the all-or-nothing thinking that they often have.

The reality is that state legislatures and family courts have established standards and rules for addressing relocation issues. It is important to find out what they are. A consultation with a lawyer can help a lot before you get started on the process of dealing with initiating or responding to a relocation request. In some states, the purpose and need for the move can be an issue. In other states, the question is simply how severe the impact will be on the other parent, and the reason for the move does not matter. Often there will be an examination of how much time each parent has traditionally spent with the child before the relocation request. And of course, the court will want to know whether the move is based on a bad faith effort to essentially eliminate the other parent from the child's life.

# Financial Manipulations

While the worst behavior of BPs, NPs, and ASPs tends to revolve around child issues in family court, they also can be highly manipulative and dishonest about financial matters. Hiding property, hiding bank accounts, filing false tax returns, withholding support payments, refusing to look for work, faking the inability to work, canceling insurance, and so forth are common issues in family court for those with these traits. Sometimes these issues accompany parenting issues, but sometimes there are no children and these personalities still find their way into family court battles over financial manipulations.

## False Allegations of Financial Manipulations

Of course, the other side of doing these behaviors is accusing the other party of engaging in them. This is an area where record keeping becomes extremely important. Unlike parenting behavior, most financial transactions have a paper trail. That's why it's important from the start to copy account records, take photographs of furniture and equipment, preserve emails and text messages, and otherwise keep track of your family's financial situation.

# Conclusion

All of these issues create situations in which organizing and presenting the facts of the case and the blamer's patterns of behavior are very important. Keeping a written record of your actions and efforts in this regard will help you if you end up in court on any of the issues in this chapter.

# Chapter 8

# Hiring a Lawyer Who Understands

Selecting the right lawyer may be your single biggest decision. Interview at least three attorneys before choosing the one you want to retain as your advocate through what may be the roller-coaster ride of a lifetime. Ideally, look for an attorney who:

- Has experience in your court: Your attorney should know the judges and what to expect in their courtrooms. There is some variation among counties, so find a local attorney who knows the local rules and is respected by your judge.

- Is easy to communicate with: Your attorney should be open to your input and concerns and plan to work closely with you in handling surprises and legal maneuvers.

- Understands difficult personalities in family court cases: While you may not find an attorney with specific knowledge of BP, NP, and ASP traits, some are better than others at handling common manipulations and false statements.

Few attorneys recognize and understand PDs. They simply view blamers as jerks, liars, or incredibly frustrating opponents. If you find an attorney who is experienced in your court, is easy to communicate with, is open-minded, returns your phone calls, and is willing to share decision making with you, you may be able to educate him on the personality issues. Keep in mind that most family law attorneys are reluctant to take potentially high-conflict cases, because blamers drain their energy, too.

Using referral sources, such as the following ones, is more effective than making cold calls from the phone book. After getting names, be sure to interview the lawyers yourself.

- Mental health professionals: Contact a mental health professional who knows about PDs and works on family law cases. Psychologists, clinical social workers, and family counselors regularly testify in court or do assessments for the court.

- Mental health organizations (such as a psychiatric hospital or counseling clinic): Explain your situation to someone who has dealt with people with BP, NP, or ASP traits, then ask if the person has referrals to three attorneys.

- Family and friends: Someone you know may have had a good experience with an attorney in a difficult case. Keep in mind that the case may have been quite different from yours.

- Referral service: Many county bar associations have referral services that usually give out three names. Then you can interview all three and make a choice.

- Court observation: If you've got the time, go to the court where your case will be heard and observe the attorneys. See the way they interact with each other and argue their cases. If you like one, go up afterward and ask for a business card.

Clerks at court are not supposed to give legal advice, but they're familiar with the attorneys who regularly come to court. Sometimes they will give you hints about who's good and whom to avoid. You might ask a clerk, "If I had to choose between so-and-so and what's-her-name, whom would you suggest?"

## What to Ask

There's a wide range of attorneys; you'll want to find one who fits you like a partner, accompanying you through the ups and downs of what will likely be an unpleasant journey. Here are some critical questions to ask:

**How do you usually communicate with clients?** Look for answers that include a usual response time for returning phone calls of at least twenty-four to forty-eight hours, depending on the urgency of the issue. You don't want an attorney who will always pass you off to an assistant, associate, or secretary. Sometimes staff will be able to help you, which saves you money. Just make sure you have access to your lawyer when you need it.

Ask how easy it is to schedule an appointment with the attorney when you want to discuss your case. When you speak with a prospective attorney, notice whether she is distracted by other matters (phone calls, papers to review, and so on). Does she seem attentive? Is the attorney a good listener, or does he interrupt or take over the conversation before you explain your concerns?

There will be times when your attorney is unavailable, so ask who will be available instead or when email communication is usually read. Remember, when your case is going to court, you'll want your attorney to be just as absorbed in it as you are and less available to others. If you feel good about the communication, the relationship may work.

**Do you prefer to negotiate or go to court? About how many cases have you settled this year? About how many cases have you taken to court for hearings or trials?** While negotiations may work, many attorneys quickly become frustrated with blamers' rigid thinking, mood swings, arrogance, and disrespect. These attorneys may try to avoid this mess by prematurely ending negotiations. That's not what you want. You want a lawyer who won't take these behaviors personally and will exhaust all settlement options before going to court. But a credible threat of going to court sometimes helps settle a case, so be sure to hire a lawyer who is equally competent in and out of court.

When you use the same attorney for court whom you used in negotiations, that person will be familiar with you and with the other side's manipulations, allegations, and rigid thinking. Patterns of behavior that occurred in negotiations (which will probably escalate in court) may help your attorney plan a winning strategy.

**Have you ever handled a case like mine before?** Ideally, the answer is yes. Some attorneys may have had lots of experience with your type of case, and others will be relatively new. Experience matters a lot in law, because there are so many details, rules, and tools you'll use. It's helpful if the attorney is familiar with your judge and how your judge handles cases like yours.

If you like an attorney, but he doesn't have much experience with high-conflict cases, ask the attorney if he has a colleague or mentor with whom he may consult. Sometimes a new attorney will spend a lot more time on your case just for the learning experience. This may benefit you if the person has a more experienced attorney available for consultation who will point the newer attorney in the right direction. A more experienced attorney will know what tools to use in handling your case and may have some legal research and documents she has used from similar cases she recently handled.

**What steps would you take in handling a case like mine?** There is no right answer to this question. Mostly, you want to see if the attorney's steps make sense to you and if she explains things to your satisfaction. This will give you an idea of whether the attorney is familiar with the common problems of persuasive blamers or whether he's merely guessing. You'll also get an idea of whether you feel comfortable with this attorney's approach. Make sure this person is open to your information and suggestions.

**Do you believe that most abuse allegations are true or false?** Does the lawyer jump to conclusions about your case? Is she honest with you about her experience, her availability, and the strengths and weaknesses of your case? Beware of attorneys who readily accept any abuse allegations without question: they will turn against you in the middle of the case, when someone else makes a damaging statement against you, however false. Attorneys who are easily emotionally persuaded might suddenly change their minds rather than weigh all the evidence.

You want an attorney who doesn't presume that your abuse concerns are always true or always false. Many reasonable parents make the mistake of seeking a lawyer who is identified with one or the other extreme as a "father's rights" or "mother's rights" advocate or an advocate against abuse or against alienation. Instead, you want a skeptical lawyer who:

- Is familiar with the whole range of possibilities
- Is open-minded

- Is objective

- Asks clients lots of questions

- Seeks corroborating evidence

- Is honest with you if he thinks you're mistaken or mis-perceiving events

**What is your reputation in the legal community?** This question will show you how the attorney sees herself and what's important to her. If the lawyer brags about being ruthless, consider looking elsewhere. Judges have the most respect for problem-solver attorneys who help clients resolve their disputes.

Don't assume an aggressive lawyer is best; some have a bad reputation with the judges and may present information that's misleading or wrong. Instead, find an assertive (not aggressive) attorney who appears knowledgeable and respected by the court. Your case will be decided by a judge, not a jury, and dramatic behavior eventually falls flat in family court.

Also, look elsewhere if the attorney sees himself as a great "settler." This person may try to get you to settle a case that should be presented to a judge. Find an attorney who is known for both settlement and court experience, so she will apply the approach most appropriate to your case.

**Can you give me the names of two or three current or former clients to interview?** If you're unsure, talking to other clients may help you make a decision, but this is a delicate question; you may not want to ask unless you feel comfortable. Some attorneys will be offended; others will want to protect their clients from unnecessary intrusion. Either way, the attorney's response may tell you everything you need to know.

# What Is a Reasonable Fee?

Rates for family law attorneys range from two hundred fifty to five hundred dollars per hour, depending on your location and the attorney's years of experience. You'll need at least fifteen hundred to ten thousand dollars for a retainer for an assertive approach.

Keep in mind that your entire case may involve several hearings, possible experts, many delays, and responses to ever-escalating abusive conduct, false allegations, or both. Overall, cases range in cost from five thousand to fifty thousand dollars and sometimes higher.

If you get a good court order, you and your lawyer may have to bring the blamer back to court to enforce it—sometimes more than once. The blamer may try to reverse the order. If you get a bad court order (for example, finding you guilty of actions you never did, or the blamer is found innocent of real misbehavior), you may need to bring the case back to court. Additionally, even after the divorce is over, new issues may inspire the blamer to bring you back to court, or you may need the court to set limits on new, unwanted behaviors.

The cost of the attorney should not be the deciding factor in your selection. Attorneys with high fees may not necessarily pay the most attention to your case. A lower-cost attorney may have the right qualifications and be more committed.

# Can You Get By with a Consulting Attorney?

Consulting attorneys usually don't represent their clients in court (although they may do so on request). Instead, they explain the law and court procedures to guide their clients. If you are thinking of trying to represent yourself in family court, we strongly recommend that you at least have a consulting attorney. Since more and more people are representing themselves in family court these days despite the high risks, this may be a helpful alternative for you. If you take this approach, a consulting attorney can help you:

- Develop negotiation strategies to stay out of court

- Prepare documents (or do it for you)

- Conduct legal research (or do it for you)

- Help you practice what to say in court

If you take this route, be sure to hire a consulting attorney who can switch to representing you if you get in over your head or if your blamer makes false allegations or starts to misbehave—a distinct possibility.

*Sarah found an attorney she feels comfortable with, Brett. According to Sarah's therapist, Brett has a good reputation. It's true that he doesn't know much about PDs, but he seems open to being educated and will listen to her concerns. He says that Sarah's husband's attorney is usually open to negotiations. In this situation, the attorneys may be able to work together to minimize the conflict and do what is right, even though they don't understand the dynamics of blamers with BP, NP, or ASP traits.*

*Thomas has been fortunate to find an attorney, Karen, who is familiar with abuse and false allegations of abuse. She also knows about blamers in family court cases. But the lawyer for Thomas's borderline soon-to-be ex-wife Tammy has no interest in working with Karen and hasn't checked out Tammy's claims. (More about the common characteristics of this type of attorney will be explained in chapter 11.) Thomas expects a difficult year.*

# Conclusion

Finding a good lawyer for your particular case may be the most important task, but it's not always easy. Don't expect your attorney to know much, if anything, about borderline, narcissistic, or antisocial personality disorders, but many good attorneys are familiar with dealing with high-conflict cases and managing the other side. They understand what to do, which is the most important thing.

While there are many good questions you can ask a family lawyer, keep in mind that most family law attorneys aren't really seeking more high-conflict cases because of the time and energy they can consume. So emphasize how willing you are to be helpful to your lawyer, and don't sound as if you are questioning the person's abilities. The most important issues are the lawyer's experience and ability to communicate with you.

*Chapter 9*

# Working with Your Lawyer to Handle Predictable Crises

There are many aspects to the relationship with your attorney. Being aware of them will help you work together most effectively through the chaos and frustration of a case involving a persuasive BP, NP, or ASP blamer.

## The Role of Your Attorney

Your attorney is ethically obligated to be a "zealous advocate" for you, the client. This means your attorney is required to assert your interests, maintain confidential information, and fulfill the standards of an attorney handling a case such as yours. But despite popular media, it doesn't necessarily mean the attorney can do absolutely anything on your behalf. Your attorney is also an "officer of the court." This means your attorney is an extension of the court; is trusted by the court; and is expected to act according to local court rules, state and federal laws, and numerous ethical standards. Within these dual roles, there are three primary tasks for your attorney in your court case:

- To know the law

- To gather the evidence

- To present the evidence and law to the court

In short, your attorney's role involves knowledge and strategy. Your attorney makes the technical decisions regarding which arguments to make, what evidence to use, and whether you or a witness should testify. The attorney is a case manager who may use experts and staff in an effort to accomplish your goals.

## Knowing the Law

Ask your attorney to explain legal issues so that you know what information is relevant and what isn't. Don't waste time and money talking about legally insignificant information just because it feels important or you want to vent. Know what's significant so you can provide your attorney with useful information. Sometimes it helps to have your attorney give you a copy of the law that covers the issues. This will help reassure you about what is and is not allowed. While your partner may make legal threats about custody and finances, many of them are empty threats she makes to help her feel powerful when she feels helpless. Knowing the law will help you avoid overreacting.

## Gathering Evidence

This is an area where you can be most helpful. Tell your attorney about everything that might be relevant to your case, and don't be offended if much of it is irrelevant. But sometimes one little insignificant piece of information opens up a valuable new area of inquiry. Ask your attorney to review what information you've gathered.

If you have lots of papers (journal notes about your parenting and your partner's behavior, numerous bank statements, letters and emails, and prior court records), organize them by category and provide a one- to two-page summary explaining how they help your case.

Ask whether you should obtain declarations (also known as affidavits) from people who know you. Declarations are statements signed under penalty of perjury that provide specific information about key issues relevant in your case. If your blamer says your children are afraid of you and you believe they are not, then you should provide statements from people who have observed you with your children, along with a specific description of what they observed. Opinions or statements that say you're a really great person are not usually helpful.

Offer to do research online or at the local library. If there are piles of documents you are required to provide to the other side, or if your attorney receives piles of documents about your financial or other records, offer to sort through them for important information. This may save time for your attorney, which may save you money. Since you will always know more about the facts of your case, you may be able to point out key documents that will help settle your case or help you in court.

## Submitting Evidence to the Court

Here you must rely on your attorney's experience and knowledge of your particular case. The attorney gets to make most of the decisions in this area, but you should know what to expect. In some cases, an attorney may be willing to show you his notes for presentation of evidence and arguments, so that you can provide useful additions or last-minute clarifications. It can help to organize brief summaries of useful information for your lawyer as she is preparing, as you know the facts of the case better than anyone. Your lawyer will know what is relevant and permissible as evidence. Ask your lawyer how you can be helpful with this.

# The Role of the Client

Of course, your role is to make the big decisions, such as whether to make a settlement offer, whether to accept a settlement offer, whether to have a hearing, what issues to take to court, whether to go to trial, whether to appeal, and whether to keep or change your attorney. Don't get into power struggles with your attorney about these issues. Try to develop a collaborative relationship so that you both can keep an open mind.

The attorney must inform you about the implications of these decisions and provide all relevant information available to her. An attorney must keep you apprised of developments in the case, including all settlement offers, even if the attorney thinks they are absurd or will be rejected.

Discuss these matters at the beginning of your relationship. Find the right balance between providing helpful information and not being a nuisance. Ask what the attorney wants you to do and not do. Be nice to your attorney; this will save you time and money. You will get more from your attorney if you have a friendly manner, thank your attorney for his hard work, and respect his boundaries. If you need to tell lawyer jokes or complain about attorneys in general, do it with your friends. Avoid attacking your attorney, regardless of how frustrated you may be. You and your attorney need to support each other. If you're not satisfied with something your attorney has done, ask to have a meeting to discuss your concerns. You may have misunderstood something, or your attorney may not have realized something. This may clear the air and improve relations. It is also important for you to understand how attorneys work on a daily basis so that your expectations are realistic and how you can be helpful to your attorney if your partner provides distortions or damaging information about you to the court.

## Understanding Your Attorney's Daily Life

One of the biggest stresses for clients and attorneys is determining how you should touch base. This is an issue because of the awkward timing and intensity of surprise events. Many family law attorneys tend to be workaholics. What you see on television and in the hallways at court may appear to be relaxed, superconfident lawyers. But behind the scenes is a lot of suppressed stress and anxiety about getting the work done and pressure to win the next case. Full-time family lawyers commonly have fifty to one hundred active and inactive cases, and any of them could flare up at any time. An old client might return with a new emergency that needs immediate attention. A current case has a new development that needs a response as soon as possible. Some documents that are due today are missing some important information.

When you call to discuss a minor point or ask a general question, the attorney may not be available or may seem very abrupt. Try not to take it personally. Ask whether this is a good time to talk. If necessary, schedule a better time to meet with the attorney. As we mentioned earlier, remember, when your case is in crisis or heading to court, you'll want your counsel's total attention.

Attorneys generally have an hourly rate and charge by the tenth of an hour (six minutes), so make your contact specific and productive while respecting your attorney's boundaries. Speak with an assistant if possible. In fact, it's very helpful to develop a positive relationship with someone in your attorney's office other than your attorney.

## Handling Distortions and Damaging Information

Blamers escalate their emotional reasoning and defensiveness when the truth comes out. They feel extremely threatened by information that contradicts their point of view. Whenever you have made progress, they will try to gain power and control by attacking you in new ways. Anticipate this, warn your attorney that this may happen, and ask to be notified right away if it does. Counter the false allegations with accurate information right away; the last thing you want is to have your attorney believe you're a child molester (for example), because she may distance herself from you.

*Larry was falsely accused of assault and battery against his wife's boyfriend during the divorce process. As evidence came out in Larry's favor, his wife dreamed up more extreme allegations. She claimed he'd been arrested and convicted in another state for the same thing—and she even named the judge. When Larry's attorney proved that the person named was never a judge, Larry's wife said she must have just remembered it wrong and that it was another judge.*

*When that story was disproved, she claimed that it all actually happened in a neighboring county. And when that was also disproved, she insisted that the necessary legal documents had been expunged after several years. When Larry's attorney proved this wasn't the policy, she changed tactics, moving on to another story involving financial allegations.*

*While these allegations may seem obvious and absurd, Larry was temporarily incarcerated because of these false allegations of assault and battery. Fortunately, Larry and his attorney understood the natural progression of these escalating allegations. They were eventually able to get the charges thrown out on appeal, but it took constant rumor control and communication between Larry and his attorney for two years to achieve this result. The wife was ultimately required to pay sanctions for misleading the court in another matter.*

If there is damaging information in your background, tell your attorney early in the case. In fact, tell your attorney anything that might look negative about you as the case progresses. If you did something embarrassing (sent a hostile email, slept with your ex, and so on), let your attorney know right away so he can do damage control.

*Thomas kept notes about his relationship with Tammy. For years, he wrote about her behavior and his ongoing frustrations. He wasn't sure if it was relevant and whether to mention it to his attorney but finally decided to ask. His attorney was enthusiastic: "Yes, journal notes could be extremely helpful, especially in showing a pattern of behavior to the evaluating psychologist. And keep making notes as the case progresses from here on. It may help us even more. But you'll need to make a brief summary for me and the psychologist. There are so many notes here it's hard to read it all."*

*Thomas's notes turned out to be one of the most helpful parts of the case, because he was able to show the evaluating psychologist the actual pattern of Tammy's mood swings, violence, and parenting difficulties. The dates and details made it credible, especially when some of it was confirmed by other, independent documents.*

## Conclusion

Communication is the most important aspect of your relationship with your lawyer. If appropriate, share this chapter with your lawyer and talk about strategy as a team. If you think it would help, you could provide your lawyer with the "Open Letter to Lawyers with Clients in Potentially High-Conflict Divorces" (find it on this book's webpage, www.newharbinger. com/46110). If you're both prepared for a roller-coaster ride, the process will be much less stressful, and both of you can focus on what's most important whenever issues arise, without constant distractions or conflicts between you.

*Chapter 10*

# Gathering Evidence About Your Blamer's Private Persona

Most people with BP, NP, or ASP traits have a public persona most people find respectful and charming (especially the court) and a private persona that's disrespectful and abusive, especially to partners (Dutton 2007; Bancroft and Silverman 2002).

Perpetrators of abuse generate false "emotional facts" that fit the court's concerns about abuse. The judge may become emotionally hooked into believing them. It isn't unusual for courts to be persuaded by this information and to get the case backward so that innocent victims are found guilty.

Ironically, blamers will tell the court that *you* have a private and manipulative persona as they project their own behavior onto you. As a target, you'll have an uphill battle. Being persistent in bringing out accurate information is key to prevailing in court. Don't hold back. Put a significant effort into obtaining factual evidence about the blamer's private persona, including evidence of prior violent acts, emotional abuse, false statements, or some combination. This may help you counter the emotional and dramatic false allegations against you, as you explain patterns to the court of the blamer's own abusive behavior and history of false statements.

# What Evidence Are You Looking For?

You are looking for three types of information:

- False statements: Get specific information about each of the blamer's allegations that is false, exaggerated, or misrepresentative.

- Pattern of abuse: Make note of patterns of the blamer's abusive behavior.

- Truth about you: Collect information that shows your true behavior and your consistent honesty.

As soon as possible, predict the most likely allegations, which are usually contained in the initial papers filed in the case. If the case starts with an emergency ex parte hearing, try to obtain the transcript after the hearing is over, so you can disprove any false or unsupported allegations. Once you know the allegations, you'll have a good idea of where to look for the evidence you'll need to submit to the court. However, some emergency hearings don't have a transcript.

## Prior Statements

The most helpful information is prior false statements made to the court or an evaluator. Judges and other court professionals don't like being lied to, so this gets their attention. You don't have to convince them your soon-to-be ex has a PD. Just demonstrate the pattern as described in chapter 14.

Blamers have a history of making inconsistent, dramatic, and false statements. They get into conflicts and may have a history of court involvement. You or your attorney should look for these court records. Perhaps your partner made the same false allegations against someone else, or perhaps he previously contradicted what he's saying now.

In one divorce case, a blamer stated that she should have custody of the child because she currently lived with a "kind and gentle man." Prior court records showed that a year earlier, she had filed a restraining order against this "gentle man" and had included photographs of the bruises. This undermined her credibility in court on all issues, and there were many issues in dispute. This was a major factor in the husband's getting custody.

## Depositions

A deposition is the process of testifying under oath while a court reporter transcribes every word. Depositions usually take place in the office of the attorney who is asking the questions. The attorney issues a deposition notice to a party or a deposition subpoena to a nonparty witness. The party or other witness is legally required to attend and answer most questions. The person testifying usually brings an attorney to give advice and make objections.

Depositions are one of the most effective tools, because blamers can be so emotional that they don't realize how they contradict themselves. A nonaggressive approach encourages them to chat. While you're legally allowed to be present, it might be helpful for you to stay away to encourage the blamer to talk more. You can be available to your attorney by phone, if needed.

A gentle approach also allows the blamer to provide carefully rehearsed speeches that supposedly explain his side of the story. Letting the blamer put his spin on the information at the start of a deposition without challenging him makes him relax and feel more confident. Then the blamer will be inclined to spin more stories that your attorney can question later on.

After the blamer has committed himself to a potentially distorted view of the target and the case, your attorney will be able to ask detailed questions in a nonthreatening, out-of-context manner so that the witness doesn't even know he has contradicted himself. Then your attorney can conduct further depositions or gather other documents that show the false statements to be untrue.

In one restraining order deposition, an ex-wife made up the story that her ex-husband had assaulted her in a shopping-center parking lot. Early in the deposition, she lied that she first saw him running up from behind her just moments before the "sudden and violent attack." But at the end of the deposition, in the context of an unrelated conversation, the now-relaxed ex-wife confirmed that she first saw her ex-husband at the store over an hour before the alleged assault and that he was gone well before the alleged assault occurred. This matched the ex-husband's story and exposed the ex-wife's statement as false.

## Declarations by Third Parties

Declarations (also known as affidavits in many jurisdictions) are written statements of fact by parties and witnesses to a case, including you and your soon-to-be ex. These statements are signed under penalty of perjury and used as a substitute for live testimony in some court hearings, saving the court time. In some cases, a witness who signs a declaration can be called to be cross-examined in court about his statements. Declarations are one of the most popular forms of evidence gathering in interpersonal disputes.

Declarations can be either extremely persuasive or almost useless. The most helpful ones are by people who objectively describe the who, what, where, and when of various events, as well as the behavior of both parties involved. Often the most credible declarations are by neutral professionals and other neutral third parties (unless they're seen as too emotionally involved).

People with BP traits may pour out their anger about feeling abandoned, focusing on many irrelevant facts about their target that don't support their extreme feelings or requests for legal intervention. People with NP traits write in a condescending manner without facts to support their superiority. People with ASP traits simply lie about a lot.

Blamers write about "emotional facts" that sound true but are false. They grab the reader's attention like rumors that grow with the telling. Some blamers consciously do this, but with others it's unconscious. Blamers experience so many painful and confusing emotions that they won't acknowledge these emotions as their own. Therefore, they blame their negative feelings on their target. Sadly, these allegations often get the attention of decision makers.

You may be tempted to respond in the same manner, but it's better to provide specific details than spew back. Focus on the facts! Avoid wild and unsupported allegations that make you look bad. Declarations that have more details and fewer value judgments and conclusions are more credible.

Reply declarations are a good way to counter false allegations. Counter each false statement item by item, with evidence of the truth. A chart that shows false statements side by side with actual facts can be of great help. But it should emphasize the most important events, rather than be a massive list of overwhelming information.

*Thomas asked his sister to write a declaration for the court and the psychological evaluator. This is what she wrote:*

> I am Thomas's sister and Tammy's sister-in-law. I have two children of my own, aged one and three. I have spent many evenings at Thomas and Tammy's home and observed both of them as parents. I have never seen Thomas inappropriately touch their daughter, Brianna. In fact, she is very comfortable

*with him and goes to him when she wants something or is upset. He rarely raises his voice with her, and when she is upset, he is effective at distracting her with an appropriate new activity, especially playing with her dolls.*

*I have observed Tammy seeming uninterested or irritated when Brianna is upset. She often prefers to watch TV or play on the computer than to pay attention to Brianna. It seems as if she automatically becomes upset when Brianna gets upset, and makes loud and angry responses to Brianna with few helpful solutions.*

*I feel very confident in Thomas's care of Brianna and his careful attention to Tammy to help her calm down when she is upset. I leave my two young children with Thomas, and many times, Tammy isn't around. I have never had any fear that he would molest my children, and I have never seen any signs of fear around him or discomfort after a visit by the children.*

*On June 4, a month before Tammy and Thomas separated, I decided not to leave my children alone with Tammy without Thomas present, because she was getting more and more moody. I have attached a copy of an email I sent to Thomas at work explaining my concerns, dated a month before their separation. I would be glad to speak to the court or anyone else about my observations and concerns.*

*This declaration is extremely helpful and credible, even though it is by Thomas's sister. She describes behavior without unnecessary emotion or opinion, describes only her personal observations, and makes no dramatic claims against Tammy. She explains her personal decisions regarding child safety and has a supporting document that gives her declaration greater credibility; her concerns about Tammy predated her declaration.*

## Declarations by Therapists

Earlier in this book, we stated that your therapist might help by writing a declaration for the court. This is a delicate area of the law. You want to be careful not to waive the confidentiality of your therapy records by making your mental health an issue in the case. Talk with your attorney first about this.

Therapists have some special dos and don'ts to consider to maintain their credibility. They should not draw conclusions or make recommendations about a person they have not met, no matter how abusive that person may have been. They may not release information about a partner who came to couples counseling, unless the partner has authorized them to do so.

A therapist who wants to help a client should write a declaration that's limited to his client's own behavior and treatment with concrete examples, as Thomas's sister did in the previous example. A credible therapist can have the greatest influence in a court case involving a blamer. Since judges are not trained in mental health issues, they rely heavily on mental health professionals.

An alternative is for therapists to give verbal input to court mediators or evaluators about your participation in therapy. This avoids the issue of writing a declaration altogether, which may be better in many situations. Then the judge sees in more vague terms what the court mediator or evaluator has written. The benefit of this approach is that it keeps your therapist farther from your legal case. The downside is that a court mediator or evaluator may write a report that misrepresents what your therapist said. As always, you should discuss this issue with your lawyer to determine the best approach.

## Documents

Documents are very persuasive in a legal case, because they appear neutral and official. Documents that show your partner's private, abusive persona may include angry emails, faxes, and letters. Blamers constantly vent their frustrated emotions to others in written form, because it's so easy these days. They impulsively express their emotions and then regret doing so.

Save these documents! They are easy to submit to the court, and they tell the story best: in the abusive person's own words. The tone of voice, the demands, and the blaming are the most convincing evidence in the case. It is hard for a blamer to claim she's a frightened, innocent victim when the court sees the angry, abusive words she uses.

NP and ASP blamers feel confident when they lie on tax returns, credit applications, and their driving records, all of which are areas where many people fudge a little. These types of blamers may lie a lot on these documents, because they believe they are entitled and won't get caught on these minor matters. Subpoenas and demands for documents may produce these records for you to examine with your attorney. Sometimes you will get the person with NP or ASP traits to sign a release for her tax records or other documents because she feels so overconfident that you won't follow through or understand what she has done. In some cases, you may need to hire an expert in document analysis.

## Recordings

Secret recordings are one of the few ways of revealing the private persona of an abusive personality. Yet they can also be illegal (depends on the state) or offend the court. Find out the rules from your attorney before you record anything. It is usually illegal to secretly record telephone conversations; in fact, it can be a federal offense, because telephone lines and signals go across state lines. Yet the courts have realized the value of such recordings in obtaining evidence of violations of restraining orders, so in some cases you may obtain a court order allowing the taping of phone calls from an abusive person.

Recording face-to-face conversations may be legal if the person making the recording is a part of the conversation. Again, check this out with your attorney.

Videotaping may be legal in some circumstances, but in others it is considered harassment and may be against the law or disallowed as evidence in court. Also, judges don't usually have the time to watch a video. In some cases, the court may prefer a transcript of a video. Family courts have been generally negative about videotaping, because presenting such evidence intrudes too much on people's right to privacy and can easily escalate conflict. In some cases, courts have allowed videotaping of visitation exchanges to monitor the behavior of parents, other parties, or both. Also, old videos or photos may be helpful in showing how comfortable and happy the children were with you as a parent, to counteract allegations that the children were always afraid of you.

## Submitting the Evidence to the Court

Not all evidence may be allowed in court. Talk to your attorney. Sometimes useful evidence about your partner's private persona isn't allowed because of privacy laws. Even people with manipulative and abusive personalities are protected from some forms of exposure.

In contrast to the impression given in the media, surprise documents or witnesses are rarely permitted. Most documents, declarations, and other forms of evidence must be submitted to the opposing party or the person's attorney by certain deadlines before a hearing or trial. Lists of witnesses, including addresses and phone numbers, must usually be provided well in advance.

Get as much information to the court and evaluators about your partner's true behavior from the start of the case, because the blamer's initial good impressions are powerful and often give him a halo effect that's hard to counteract at the last minute. When submitting evidence, though, be careful not to rely on an explosive cross-examination; it is also helpful to keep a time line of events so that you can show a pattern of behavior.

## Do Not Rely Solely on Cross-Examination

Family court isn't like what you've seen on TV or in the movies. Don't expect to win in court based on a dramatic cross-examination of the other party or her witnesses. A blamer or witness's testimony can be very unpredictable. Blamers easily mislead people with their heightened emotions. Don't give them the opportunity to work their magic on the court.

Instead, take depositions, as described at the beginning of this chapter. This way you'll find out what they are likely to say. You can challenge a witness in court with the deposition transcript if he changes his testimony. You can also consider how credible he might appear to a judge. Confronting a blamer with triggering questions may be an effective way to get her to show her angry, private persona, but it can just as easily backfire for the following reasons:

- The blamer may be so well prepared that the person asking the questions (your lawyer) looks as if he is harassing the witness.

- The testimony may sound more damaging to you.

- The blamer may be able to persuade the court that she's a victim of your aggressive campaign.

Remember, blamers (especially those with NP traits) are lifelong experts at charm, manipulation, and emotional persuasion. Don't be overconfident that you'll trap your blamer with contradictions or force him to explode on the witness stand. On the other hand, an experienced attorney may be able to elicit these responses in some cases. These decisions are best discussed with your attorney.

## Time Line

Timing of events is critical. The blamer's abusive behavior or false allegations commonly occur immediately following key times of triggering emotional events (regardless of who triggers them), such as:

- A party requests a divorce or makes a financial demand.
- A party loses a job.
- An affair is discovered.
- A former spouse gets married.
- A former spouse has a child.
- Court papers are served.

A time line of events, abuse, and allegations often shows that the blamer's actions amounted to ways to obtain power and control over an upsetting situation, rather than an objective response to a rational concern. This is one of the most common patterns of people with BP, NP, or ASP traits: a drive for power and control at moments when others gain independence or appear to gain control over them.

# Conclusion

Evidence is a yearlong course at most law schools. It is much more complicated when borderline, narcissistic, or antisocial personalities are involved, because these people have dual personas and can be so manipulative. Courts are more persuaded by strong evidence of a pattern of misbehavior (such as several false statements to the court) than by an explanation of PDs. Court is unpredictable. Work closely with your attorney from the start in determining what evidence to gather and how it should be presented to the court. Offer your lawyer any evidence you have or could obtain, and follow her advice about what would be most useful. If you seriously disagree with your lawyer about what evidence to obtain or present, get a second opinion.

## Chapter 11

# Working with Experts and Evaluators

Family courts frequently use experts as neutral court-appointed evaluators to resolve specific issues in court cases. They are used primarily to reduce the conflict and confusion of dueling experts hired separately by each party. The court also uses them because judges usually don't have special training in mental health or finances.

Evaluators can be a major part of the solution or a major part of the problem in your court case. Usually, these evaluators don't have final decision-making authority. Instead, they make reports and recommendations to the court.

Experts have specialized knowledge in areas in which the judge doesn't. Experts include mental health professionals (such as counselors and psychologists), financial experts (such as appraisers and accountants), advocates to represent someone else's interest (such as a guardian ad litem or minor's counsel for a child), or some combination.

The judges take these recommendations and make decisions after full hearings, so that each side can make formal objections and other expert opinions may be heard. But don't underestimate the importance of court-ordered evaluators. In most cases, the judges defer to their expertise, and their opinions are adopted, perhaps with some minor revisions. Therefore, if there is an evaluator, treat this person as the most influential one in the decision-making process.

## Meeting with Evaluators

Evaluators meet with the parties individually and can informally discuss the case at length, unlike the court. This wide access to evaluators allows the blamer an almost unlimited opportunity to emotionally influence the evaluator's opinion of you and significantly influence the outcome of the case. It also allows you a greater opportunity to thoroughly explain the case and the effect of the behavior patterns involved.

In cases that turn out badly, it is usually because the blamer was very aggressive with an unaware evaluator, and the target was passive, trusting that the evaluator would be objective and neutral. Evaluators are only human. It's natural to be persuaded by intense emotions. Therefore, you must be very assertive in explaining patterns of the blamer's behavior and false statements while working with evaluators, especially those with little experience with PDs in high-conflict cases.

Don't assume that the evaluator will figure out the truth without your assistance. Don't treat the evaluator as an enemy, because this may create the exact problems you wish to avoid. You need to work with the evaluator. Evaluators, especially those who are well trained and experienced in high-conflict cases, may be able to recommend the best solutions. They may also be able to keep the case from escalating further in court by resolving many, or all, of the issues out of court.

# Six General Principles for Working with Evaluators

1. **Speak with the evaluator as soon as possible.**
   Evaluators will speak directly with the parties, perhaps after an initial contact with the attorneys. Blamers will be very quick to meet with evaluators. Their goal is to team with the evaluator against you. If you speak to the evaluator at once, she should be less likely to absorb the blamer's picture of you. This doesn't mean you have to talk to the evaluator first, but if the blamer goes first, you should talk to the evaluator as soon as possible after that.

   Don't break any rules, such as contacting the evaluator too quickly or too directly. As soon as the evaluator is appointed, ask your attorney about the guidelines concerning contact with the evaluator. Follow your attorney's advice, especially if he is familiar with this particular evaluator's preferred procedures.

2. **Provide accurate, verifiable, and organized information.** Evaluators respect well-organized people. It makes their jobs easier, and when you're also organized, evaluators may identify with you. But don't appear too controlling or tell the evaluator how to do his job. Instead, submit your information in an easy-to-use format and follow the evaluator's directions about what you should do next.

   You might provide the evaluator with a set of labeled manila folders or a binder of your documents (especially if there's a lot of them) organized into four or five basic categories. Provide a one- or two-page summary or outline of the information similar to that suggested in chapter 9 for your own attorney.

One of the big mistakes that blamers make is submitting long-winded and unfocused statements, which eventually irritate most evaluators and indicate that the person has a problem. You want to be the reasonable, organized, and fact-based party.

3.   **Respond to each allegation the blamer makes about you.** Respond quickly. While the best evaluators remain neutral and don't get hooked by inflammatory allegations, it does happen, and we hear about it a lot. So find out as soon as possible what your soon-to-be ex is claiming about you. Then, right away, give the evaluator specific, factual information. Evaluators don't like to change their minds once they have reached a conclusion. They see themselves as experts and prefer not to be challenged (they're only human). Once a report has come out, many experts defend their opinions rather than take in new information.

     Anticipate your soon-to-be-ex's allegations before he makes them, and suggest at the start that you're concerned that he will make blaming statements that are dramatic, extreme, and untrue. Ask the evaluator to give you the chance to respond to any allegations right away (before she develops an opinion about you).

4.   **Meet all deadlines.** Evaluators usually set a date for submitting information. You want the evaluator to have as much fact-based information as possible before she forms her expert opinion.

5.   **Avoid complaining a lot about your case.** Unfortunately, many targets have been through so much that they spend their limited time with an evaluator complaining

about the court, other professionals, money, and the other party. None of your conversations with a court-appointed evaluator are confidential. Do your complaining with friends, family, and your own therapist.

When you complain, the evaluator may think both sides are difficult. The evaluator might make a decision that falls in between your reality and that of the blamer. Or the evaluator may think you have a difficult personality. Make the evaluator's job as easy as possible. Be friendly and stay focused. Be helpful, not a source of stress, and empathize with the evaluator's job. The evaluator will like you better and be less vulnerable to the blamer's negative attacks.

6. **Hire your own expert, if necessary.** If the court appoints an evaluator, it doesn't prevent you from seeking the services of your own expert. If you think the evaluator might be, or has been, pulled way off track by the blamer, then consider hiring your own expert. The expert may be able to prepare you for your meetings with the evaluator and complete your documents for the evaluator. In some cases, your own expert may write a formal report or speak to the court-appointed evaluator.

It's also possible to have your own expert testify in court. If your own expert is skilled at presenting testimony and expert opinions, she may be able to persuade the court that the court-appointed evaluator was incorrect on a particular issue. Successfully challenging the court-appointed evaluator after recommendations have been made is uncommon, so focus your efforts on learning how to approach your appointed evaluator well before a recommendation is written.

Make sure your expert has credible methods, a credible reputation, and, if possible, a credible history with your particular judge. Bringing in an expert who is iden-tified as extreme or always an advocate for only one side of an issue may make him useless in court.

An emotionally intense therapist who is always an advocate for victims of a certain type of abuse or always an advocate for the falsely accused may have little cred-ibility. You want someone who has a reputation for being highly objective and professionally cautious. The judge will particularly appreciate hearing about the unique factors of your case from an objective point of view.

If possible, find an expert who is familiar with your court system and your judge. In some cases, you might ask your court-appointed evaluator for a recommenda-tion of an expert for you to talk to separately. Of course, the evaluator may not help you because he may see that as violating his neutrality or as a challenge to him. But it's worth a try in some cases.

If your attorney doesn't know of an expert on your issue (parenting, finances, and so on), ask her to speak to court personnel to find out which psychological experts appear in court these days and are respected by the judge. These court personnel might include a fellow attorney, a bailiff, or a court clerk in the court's busi-ness office. Professional organizations may have referrals as well.

Once you've selected an expert, ask this person for a realistic assessment of your case. Be frank about any issues you might have and see whether the expert has any recommendations for working on any of your own issues, if there is a question about your own mental health. If your expert believes you've got some issues to work on, discuss how to handle those issues. The courts respect and encourage people who acknowledge that they have a drug or anger problem and are getting treatment for it. Start as soon as possible.

Your own expert may be able to help you respond to false allegations with more information. She may interpret psychological data that isn't always clear-cut and that may not be as bad as it appears to the nonprofessional. This is especially important if you're concerned that an evaluator has become biased against you. Your own expert may be able to counterbalance some of those negative opinions.

# Understanding the Different Types of Evaluators

The following sections contain some general information. Talk with your attorney about the laws specific to your state.

## Court Counselors

In disputes over children in ordinary divorces, child-abuse cases, and guardianship cases, the parties are usually required to meet with mental health professionals (usually family therapists or clinical social workers) before the judge hears the case. These mental health professionals are sometimes called *family court counselors* or *family court mediators*.

In many cases, these counselors act as evaluators who will make specific recommendations about parenting plans. In many states, about 90 percent of the time a custody evaluator's recommendations are adopted by the judge. Therefore, evaluators are extremely powerful. Treat this person as the primary decision maker in your case and prepare yourself for what you tell her.

When the court provides these evaluators, there is usually no charge or a minimal charge. But they usually have only one to two hours to decide your whole parenting plan. The court assigns the counselor; you don't get to pick one. While most of these counselors are good, you never know whom you'll get. There is some risk of getting a counselor who is easily hooked by a blamer.

One client of Bill's reported that the counselor wouldn't look him in the eye from the start, after reading the blamer's allegations against him. It took a lot of work and factual information to overcome that counselor's recommendations. But he did.

You can usually challenge the counselor's recommendations, including gathering more information and cross-examining the counselor at a hearing or trial. This may be a case in which you want to have your own expert testify. If children are involved in the divorce, the evaluator's parenting plan, if adopted, will become a precedent that may be very difficult to change later. While most parenting decisions can be modified throughout the child's life when circumstances change, court decisions pick up a momentum of their own. They become hard to modify unless a new change of circumstances is compelling.

## Private Counselors

An alternative is to agree on a private counselor to help resolve parenting issues. While private custody counselors often have more experience than the court's counselors, this will cost money (if your county has family court counselors, they are usually free). But private counselors may have unlimited time to become familiar with your case and to recognize the blamer's behavior patterns. In the future, you may be able to return to this person to try to make agreements so that you can stay completely away from court.

# Psychologists

When mental health issues are serious and important, the court may order a psychological evaluation. Psychologists are perhaps the most often appointed evaluators in high-conflict court cases today. They evaluate restraining order, criminal, civil court, probate court, and family court cases.

Psychologists can do a more extensive evaluation of a family to determine the best parenting plan in a particular case. They perform psychological tests to determine issues that may impair parenting skills. Psychologists can explain what's going on in a high-conflict or confusing case. They can make detailed recommendations.

The psychological testing indicates patterns of unconscious thoughts and behaviors. This is harder to manipulate than simple direct questioning. Tests may uncover lying, harmful behaviors, and the existence of a PD. But they generally resist saying that either party has a personality disorder, because they fear it will influence the decision maker too much. That's why presenting patterns is more effective. Of course, such testing will reveal your own characteristics as well, since we all usually have some areas of vulnerability or need for growth.

Psychological evaluators are ethically required to obtain information from many sources, not just from psychological testing or from the parties themselves. By gathering information from different sources, they have the opportunity to put together the most comprehensive analysis of your case.

In many cases, the psychologist's report is a very helpful tool. Many cases are settled without further appearances at court after the psychologist's recommendations are received. Unfortunately, psychologists are also human. From time to time, even psychologists get hooked by blamers and become influenced or misled by their emotions and misinformation—especially when blamers with antisocial personalities are involved.

## Attorneys for Minor Children

Many courts appoint an attorney or guardian ad litem for the children in a difficult case. Attorneys for the minor children are known by different names in different states, including *friend of the court* and *court-appointed special advocate* (CASA). In some cases, the child's advocate is not an attorney but a trained volunteer. Regardless of the details of their roles, attorneys for minor children may be the key to resolving your case. While they are technically not evaluators, the same suggestions apply to dealing with attorneys for minor children as for all other evaluators described in this chapter.

The tasks are somewhat different for attorneys for minor children. Unlike other evaluators, they usually appear in court, but they cannot be cross-examined on the witness stand because they're attorneys for a party in the case. Their reports can be more powerful than counselors' or psychologists', since judges consider attorneys to be most familiar with the rules of evidence, legal issues, and legal terminology. Or they may not be allowed to file a report and just give a verbal presentation.

An attorney for minor children may appear regularly before the judge, so it isn't uncommon for a judge to say, "If Mr. Smith says it, I believe it. I am very familiar with his work." This is less true in regard to counselors and psychologists, who are thoroughly questioned on the witness stand when they appear in court, although their expert knowledge may ultimately decide the case.

One of the benefits of attorneys for minor children is that they go out and actually do fact finding on location. They visit parents' homes, meet with teachers, and may speak directly with Child Protective Services workers and therapists. They gather information from different sources, just like psychological evaluators do.

While the psychological evaluator tries to see what's under the public persona by using psychological testing, an attorney for minor children actually observes parents and relatives at home in their normal environments, where they're more likely to show their impulsive anger and disdain for the other parent. Of course, the most manipulative blamers keep their charming public personas going almost all the time.

## Appraisers

There are many kinds of appraisers: home value appraisers, household furniture appraisers, family business appraisers, and so forth. The role of an appraiser is to come up with a financial value for an asset that is to be divided in the divorce. This is an important process that can be complicated, so discuss it with your lawyer. Blamers often have overly high expectations of the value of assets and are unwilling to accept disappointment. They may desperately try to influence an appraiser. It's possible that the appraiser may be called as a witness in court to testify about the value of a home, an unusual vehicle, the furniture, or a business.

Appraisers usually issue reports with the value they have determined and the basis for it. These reports often include comparable values for similar homes, vehicles, or businesses, which you can investigate and challenge, if necessary. But it's better to have as much contact with the appraiser as the blamer has from the start, because the blamer may blame you for peripheral, unrelated things that influence the appraiser on values that have wiggle room.

In one divorce case, the parties walked through the house together with a furniture appraiser, each saying whether an item was separate or community property. Many items were disputed, and the appraiser duly noted each of their opinions. Then the husband had to leave early. As he looked back at the house, the husband noticed his blamer wife leaning close to the appraiser, touching his arm, and telling him what a wonderful job he was doing. The report came out heavily in her favor, and the appraiser made an unrelated comment that the husband had been hostile toward the wife, which did not appear to be true and was certainly irrelevant to the value of the furniture. But it was the type of comment that helped the blamer give the husband a negative stereotype with the judge, which had to be overcome later in the case.

## Accountants

When a divorce involves a family business, the appraiser is usually a forensic accountant who is used to determining the "marital value" of the business in a divorce. This is done to determine the financial interest of the spouse who will no longer be involved. While the accountant may focus on interpreting documents and numbers, he may also meet separately with each party. The impression each party makes can affect his recommendations. Blamers may tell the accountant that you have engaged in all kinds of bad business behavior, whether or not you and your spouse are both involved in the business. Foster a positive relationship with the accountant and encourage her to ask you questions about the business, whether you or your spouse is the managing party.

Blamers have three common cognitive distortions based on their all-or-nothing thinking (splitting) regarding family businesses, and they're ready to blame you for them. First, if a partner with NP traits is the one operating the business, he is likely to say that you have no rights to any value that was created in "my business." He will say it's all his. The laws in most states say that both parties have the right to share the value that was created in a business during the marriage. The partner with NP traits may say that it has no family value or its debts are more than its assets, which is sometimes true. But you should make no assumptions and ask for more information.

Second, suddenly at the time of the divorce, many partners with NP traits say they plan to quit working in the business. People with narcissistic personalities don't like sharing or being investigated. Don't get rattled by these claims. These people rarely actually quit, and the courts may still divide the business according to its value at the time of separation. Talk to your attorney about these threats and ask the accountant to explain the finances of the business to you, until you have an accurate picture of the business.

Third, if you're the spouse operating a family business and the other party has BP traits, she may be angry and suspicious. People with borderline personalities expect to be taken care of for life, regardless of divorce laws. She may have unrealistic expectations that the business is worth a lot more than it is. If the business has little value, she may believe you've hidden its income or purposely run it into the ground. In other words, it's all your fault!

Of course, some people do hide income and run their businesses into the ground, so the court will not disregard these concerns, even if they don't fit your case. Getting a neutral, court-appointed forensic evaluation may really help explain the true status of your business. It's worth trying to persuade the other party to jointly agree to this without resorting to a court hearing.

## Special Masters

Sometimes the court assigns a specific issue or set of small issues to a special master. This person may be involved in a wide variety of issues, including custody and visitation, furniture division, and determination of the value and assignment of assets involving millions of dollars. The special master evaluates each issue and usually makes a recommendation to the court, which usually adopts her recommendation. Stay on top of any allegations, especially if the special master isn't familiar with high-conflict court cases. As always, provide specific, fact-based information and respond to allegations right away.

There was a special master in a divorce case in which a narcissistic ex-husband was angry about his ex-wife's request for more child support after his income substantially increased—a fairly ordinary and reasonable request. Since child support is based on guidelines, there wasn't any way he was going to avoid this increase. Instead, he claimed the ex-wife owed him money from the sale of a residence ten years prior. The judge was uncertain and appointed a special master. The special master got emotionally hooked by the ex-husband's allegations and submitted a report stating that the ex-wife still owed him money.

Fortunately, the ex-wife came up with a mountain of ten-year-old documents countering the false allegations. Then, the special master changed his findings and said that the matter had been resolved. This is an example of the common retaliation by people with NP traits whenever a request or demand is made of them (because they don't feel in control, and their superiority feels at risk). Don't be surprised by such shenanigans, even when you make a reasonable request.

## Obtaining an Evaluator

Your attorney may know who is a good evaluator in regard to any specific subject. Do your own research about whom to propose as an evaluator, after clearing it with your attorney. Look online, ask friends or your therapist, or find people who had similar cases to your own. Be a helpful source of ideas, but defer to your attorney and avoid confrontation. Your goal is to have a list of three names you both feel comfortable with, to present to the judge or to the other side for possible agreement to potentially avoid a court hearing.

*A few weeks before their trial date, Sarah, Sam, and their attorneys received the evaluator's custody report and recommendations. Following up on the psychological evaluator's strong request, they read the report but didn't keep a copy. That way, Sarah and Sam wouldn't be tempted to spread the highly evaluative feedback to family and friends.*

*The evaluator reported that though Sarah had experienced some mild depression off and on during her life, this was not a problem and she was not presently depressed. She sought a therapist on her own and had built a good support system. There was no evidence of her leaving pills around their son, and even Sam was unable to be specific about the allegation he had made at the first hearing.*

*The evaluator stated that though Sam was a caring father, he was self-absorbed and found others to watch their son, Jay, while he was busy. In the three months since they had separated, he had become involved with a woman who cared for the child more than he did.*

*The evaluator reported that Jay appeared to be more closely bonded with Sarah and that she was better able to soothe him and provide full attention to him than Sam was. Therefore, the evaluator recommended that Sarah have primary physical custody and that Sam have frequent visits for two hours on Mondays, Wednesdays, and Fridays and two hours on alternate Saturdays until Jay was older.*

*The evaluator had recommended to Sam early in the evaluation that he have a substance-abuse assessment. Sam had not followed up on the recommendation, and the evaluator recommended that Jay not spend overnights or long periods of time with Sam until he did so.*

*Now that the parties had their evaluation report, they would need to decide how to handle it at the coming trial. Sarah agreed with the report's recommendations, but Sam and his attorney disagreed.*

## Should an Expert Testify About BPD or NPD?

Given the general lack of awareness of PDs in today's courts, this is a common question—and a complicated one. If you're too aggressive about raising this subject, the judge may be angry with you for seeming to attack someone's personality, as described throughout this book. Yet if the judge doesn't fully understand the personality dynamics beneath the surface, he may misunderstand your case and get it backward. Getting the right balance requires a good deal of finesse.

Don't use the term "personality disorder" in court unless someone else brings it up. Explain patterns of behavior to evaluators and to the judge by providing detailed, accurate examples. Then explain why you're concerned that these patterns of behavior are not going to change unless there is court intervention (sanctions, restraining orders, changes in the parenting plan, and so forth).

Ideally, the psychological evaluator will explain BPD, NPD, or ASPD in her report. Then the judge will decide whether she believes these dynamics exist and what court orders are needed in response. But the evaluator may not mention these disorders at all. Psychologists and other mental health professionals traditionally resist believing that PDs are important in family court discussions. They fear that one party will use it as a weapon against the other. They also don't believe that the existence of a PD (or traits) should, in and of itself, determine who should have custody or visitation. But you can provide evidence of their patterns of behavior. For example, with BPD there may be two different types of patterns, as shown in the following chart.

## People with BPD with Overlapping Characteristics

| | Mostly Lower-Functioning Conventional BPs | Mostly Higher-Functioning Invisible BPs |
| --- | --- | --- |
| Coping Techniques | *Acting In:* Mostly self-destructive acts such as self-harm. | *Acting Out:* Uncontrolled and impulsive rages, criticism, and blame. These may result less from a lack of interpersonal skills (more typical of conventional BPs) than from an unconscious projection of their own pain onto others. |
| Willingness to Obtain Help | Self-harm and suicidal tendencies often bring these BPs into the mental health system (both as inpatients and outpatients). High interest in therapy. | A state of denial much like an untreated alcoholic. Disavows responsibility for relationship difficulties, refuses treatment; when confronted, accuses others of having BPD. May see a therapist if threatened but rarely takes it seriously or stays long. |

|  | Mostly Lower-Functioning Conventional BPs | Mostly Higher-Functioning Invisible BPs |
|---|---|---|
| Co-occurring (Concurrent) Mental Health Issues | Mental conditions such as bipolar and eating disorders require medical intervention and contribute to low functioning. | Concurrent illness is most commonly a substance use disorder or another personality disorder, especially narcissistic personality disorder. |
| Functioning | BPD and associated conditions make it difficult to live independently, hold a job, manage finances, and so on. Families often step in to help. | Appears normal, even charismatic, to outsiders but exhibits BP traits behind closed doors. May have a career and be successful. |
| Impact on Family Members | Major family focus on practical issues such as finding treatment, preventing/reducing self-destructive behavior, and providing practical and emotional support. Parents feel extreme guilt and are emotionally overwhelmed. | Without an obvious illness, family members blame themselves for relationship problems and try to get their emotional needs met. They make fruitless efforts to persuade the person with BP to get professional help. Major issues include high-conflict divorce and custody cases. |

A lack of knowledge about BPD, NPD, and ASPD may make it difficult to communicate the seriousness of these disorders to the court, especially:

- Why there is danger that might not be obvious

- Why these people's statements about themselves are so highly unreliable

- Why their statements about you are so highly unreliable

- Why they often won't follow court orders

If the evaluator doesn't report these terms or patterns sufficiently, it may be helpful to hire an expert of your own, as we described earlier in this chapter, to explain these unchanging patterns of behavior and possibly explain BPD, NPD, and ASPD using those terms. Your own expert can give a critique of the evaluator's report in court and point out that the patterns of behavior that have been described through your examples add up to a possible PD and, therefore, various predictable problems.

Before your expert testifies, your attorney and the expert can discuss how to present these patterns and future possible problems, with or without using the terms BPD, NPD, or ASPD. Your attorney might ask: Did you see a pattern of angry outbursts and mood swings? Could such a pattern be harmful to the child if it continues? Is this a common pattern of behavior recognized by mental health professionals? What is it called? What are the implications for parenting with this pattern of behavior? How likely is this behavior to change? (In fact, your attorney should first ask these same questions of the evaluator at a hearing or trial, then decide whether your own expert needs to testify.)

Remember that the most effective experts are those who have a good reputation with the judge. While some evaluators may not want to strongly criticize their colleagues, there may be others who are willing to respectfully disagree. It is much better to find an expert familiar to your court than to use an outside expert solely to explain BPD, NPD, or ASPD. Such "outsiders" are usually not given much credibility by family court judges (even though they might be used to persuade juries in criminal court cases, such as seen on TV and in the movies).

# Conclusion

If an evaluator is required or agreed on, focus your full attention on this aspect of the case. In reality, the evaluator is usually the primary decision maker, because judges usually respect the time evaluators put into a full investigation and their knowledgeable recommendations.

Many cases are peacefully and efficiently resolved through the use of court-appointed evaluators. If you want to keep the case out of court or minimize your time there, discuss having a neutral, court-appointed evaluator. The judge will usually agree that this is a good approach, even if your partner objects. Once the evaluator has sufficiently analyzed the facts and made a recommendation, the parties may settle the case out of court, making a full court hearing unnecessary.

Yet when BP, NP, or ASP traits are involved, be prepared for your partner to totally reject an unfavorable evaluation and press for a court hearing or a new evaluator. Don't be surprised if the evaluator becomes emotionally hooked by the blamer and reaches a bizarre or opposite conclusion. Evaluators sometimes inadvertently become emotionally biased because of the blamer's intense emotions. If this occurs, we strongly recommend that you obtain your own expert as we described. But from the start, try to make sure your relationship with the evaluator is as good as the information you provide.

# Chapter 12

# What to Expect from the Blamer's Attorney

When blamers with borderline or narcissistic personalities go to court, they escalate their emotions, their aggressive energy, and their allegations against you. The most aggressive blamers go to court to seek validation of their cognitive distortions, revenge for perceived abandonment (people with BP traits) or perceived insults to their superiority (people with NP traits), or an opportunity for manipulation (people with ASP traits). They know that court is an adversarial process, and they seek an attorney who knows how to manipulate the system with only one goal in mind: winning at any cost.

A BP blamer wants a lawyer who will be a "hero" to protect him and get revenge for your "abandonment" (even if he broke up with you). An NP blamer wants "the best," someone who will match her own self-perceived superiority. An ASP blamer wants a shark who will humiliate or destroy you. These types of blamers often shop for an attorney with a reputation for being a jerk to the other side. They want someone who won't challenge their cognitive distortions and will agree with them and reinforce their angry emotions. And, as one blamer with antisocial traits said before hiring an attorney to file her false allegations,

"Court is a liar's club. The best liar wins!" After getting caught, she was sanctioned by the court at the end of her case, to teach her that she was wrong.

Often a blamer's lawyer will make your life miserable (and your lawyer's life miserable) with escalating claims but little or no research about their basis in fact, frequent legal threats, piles of documents and demands for documents, highly emotional letters and declarations about you, depositions, and numerous unnecessary hearings. You may feel stalked and harassed. Yet all of this is legal in an effort to "discover" the truth. If you're prepared for this possibility, you can fight back.

# Two Types of Opposing Attorneys

The deciding factor in how difficult your case will become is usually the opposing attorney. Most attorneys fall into two types: "problem solvers" and "negative advocates." Both of these types may get emotionally hooked and believe their client's cognitive distortions at first. Negative advocates consistently escalate the conflict and emotions in the case, while problem solvers make efforts to reduce the emotions and level of conflict and to focus on fact finding and solving problems. (See the explanation of negative advocates in chapter 3 and the charts in the middle of chapter 6 on contributing roles in high-conflict divorce that compare emotional persuasion to fact finding.)

## Handling Problem-Solver Attorneys

Professional and ethical, problem-solver attorneys are the largest group of attorneys—although the negative advocates get the most media attention. Problem solvers fit the traditional mold of those who are honest and proud of their profession and who really want to solve problems. They also can be friendly, businesslike, and open to new ideas. They will discuss and encourage negotiations, but will usually go to court if necessary.

This type of attorney can be effective at managing their clients, including people with BP, NP, or ASP traits, but if a problem-solver attorney tries too hard to control a blamer, she may get fired, and the blamer will seek an attorney who better fits his dysfunctional needs.

Your attorney may get crisis calls from a problem-solver attorney who represents your partner, the opposing party. But this opposing attorney may try to dispense with crises as quickly as possible, to move on to problem solving. In an effort to defuse the conflict, she may say, "Who really knows who's telling the truth. Maybe both parties are lying. We probably both have difficult clients."

Problem solvers are used to seeing conflict as a mutual affair. Many family law problem-solver attorneys are learning about the dynamics of domestic violence, child abuse, parental alienation, and false allegations, so now many understand that it may just be one party who has a serious problem in some cases. While few are aware of the dynamics of PDs, many are beginning to recognize the patterns in their "difficult client" cases.

Over time, the crisis calls and letters from a problem-solver attorney may subside, and she may become more skeptical of the blamer's absurd claims. Your attorney may even point out to the opposing attorney, "Each time your client has a crisis, it turns out to be unfounded or a nonemergency. You might tell your client he has lost credibility with me, and I will no longer rush to contact my client to discuss your complaints."

*Early in their case, Sam's attorney called Sarah's attorney, urgently stated that Sarah had cleaned out a joint bank account, and demanded immediate corrective action. Sarah proved to her attorney that this had not occurred, and her attorney passed on the information. With the next crisis, Sam's attorney merely sent an email stating: "My client says your client is angry and won't return the child on time after her visitation. Please remind your client to do so." Sarah had returned the child on time before her attorney even got in touch with her. Her attorney knew by then that she was being reliable and that this was an overreaction or a knowingly false allegation by Sam.*

*After that, Sarah's attorney just received ordinary letters from Sam's attorney, raising issues "of potential concern," but not raising them as crises. The conflicts reduced in this case, because both attorneys were problem solvers who actively resisted the intense targeting of each other's client.*

*While Sarah's attorney was tempted to attack back, he stayed focused on solving the immediate problem with information rather than a battle of blame. Sarah learned to feel safe with his assertive approach.*

## Handling Negative-Advocate Attorneys

As explained in chapter 3, negative advocates are people who advocate for the blamer's cognitive distortions and join in her distortion campaigns against the target. They often believe everything the blamer says about being a helpless victim, and they may become aggressive in trying to help. They get emotionally "hooked."

Anyone can be a negative advocate if they assist a blamer in this manner. Some people are habitual negative advocates, including some lawyers. They represent as true whatever their clients say, with little or no skepticism or investigation. This is like representing a drunk while he's still under the influence, accepting what he says as the truth and justifying his bad behavior.

Negative-advocate attorneys escalate their cases and take most of their case activity to court. They formally adopt a splitting approach, acting as if their client does no wrong and you do no right. You'll hear about the smallest error on your part, while the negative advocate defends her client's major misconduct. Under the guise of legal advocacy, this type of attorney will excuse his client's unnecessary and expensive abusive behavior, harassment, and legal maneuvers.

Some negative advocates are well known to the judges, while others stay under the radar, especially with new judges. They often take more opportunities to become familiar to the judges, and thus they may have an advantage over an attorney who is new or rarely appears in court. Sometimes the judge may assume the negative advocate is more familiar with the law and is an advocate of true victims who need vigorous representation. Negative advocates turn most of their cases into "my client is an extreme victim" cases, regardless of the facts. Many are known for turning small, simple cases into large, expensive court battles.

Not surprisingly, negative-advocate attorneys are appealing to blamers. They like such attorneys' aggressive manner, their blind acceptance of the blamer's allegations, and their willingness to take almost any case to court. They like the negative advocate's drive to intimidate you and your attorney. Just to get it over with, many parties and attorneys settle their cases with negative-advocate attorneys—which simply encourages them.

Some problem-solver attorneys refuse to take cases with a well-known negative advocate on the other side. Most problem solvers learn how to manage negative advocates in ways similar to those described in this book.

With a negative-advocate attorney, there may be numerous emergency hearings, most over minor issues, absurd claims, or events that never happened. But the court doesn't know this. With little time for you and your attorney to gather and present factual information, the negative-advocate attorney may succeed in persuading the court to take some of these claims seriously, and the court may make emergency orders that are totally baseless. Much of your case may be spent undoing the damage done in these early hearings.

To help prevent these hearings from harming you, prepare for a court battle from the start (see chapter 5), and be ready to quickly respond with factual information (as described in chapter 6).

These highly aggressive attorneys often don't win in the long run. In fact, research shows that assertive attorneys do just as well as aggressive attorneys in terms of the outcome of the case (Rieke and Stutman 1990). It's just that aggressive attorneys are more dramatic and look more successful on the surface.

Some negative-advocate attorneys give brilliant performances in family court, but their dramatic speeches may manipulate the facts and the law. People watching may think they are the "best" attorneys, certainly the most confident and dramatic. The average observer doesn't see that the negative-advocate attorney may lose the next hearing, because the opposing attorney presents more facts and a strong defense. Sometimes the negative-advocate attorney is no longer on the case at future hearings, either because he had a disagreement with his blamer client (now he's to blame) or his client can't afford his high fees anymore. Blamers who hire negative advocates often bond and break up with several attorneys over the course of the case. Some of their new attorneys may not be negative advocates (which may bring you hope), but the blamer may still fire them because they are realistic and reasonable.

# Inflammatory Letters and Declarations

Blamers share their intense feelings with their attorneys, sparking one of three responses:

- The attorney tries to confront them and discourage their blame.

- The attorney tries to placate them by agreeing with their blame.

- The attorney agrees with them and escalates their blame.

Attorneys are paid to advocate for their clients. Therefore, many attorneys for blamers simply accept their allegations as true and act on them with little or no verifying research. Thus, even prior to arguing their cases in court, they may promote their clients' allegations in letters and declarations. It satisfies their clients and doesn't take much work.

Many attorneys write letters to you or your attorney containing harsh commentaries on you and your alleged misbehaviors. Your attorney may say to simply ignore them, because they don't show up in court and they have no legal significance. But you may still think you need to respond and defend yourself to persuade the opposing attorney that his client is lying or being misleading.

Declarations that rant and rave without factual basis are increasingly unpopular with the courts. Your attorney may tell you not to worry; the other attorney probably doesn't believe it either and is just writing the letter for his client's benefit. He may say the judge doesn't see these inflammatory letters, so they don't deserve a response.

Whether to respond to these letters is a question of judgment. Responding may just escalate the problem, while ignoring them may calm things down, but your attorney may need to respond to confront the other attorney with the facts. While it might feel emotionally satisfying to have your attorney respond with anger, such strong responses can inspire even stronger replies. So carefully assess the situation and determine whether the best approach may be to leave things alone or write an assertive letter in response, one that just says that the statements are untrue or exaggerated, but ends on a calming note. This depends on the issue, whether it's likely to end up in court, and whether the opposing attorney is a negative advocate or a problem solver.

When the opposing attorney files declarations with the court, you should almost always respond with your own declaration explaining the facts. You don't want a court record that just includes the other side's allegations. Have your attorney file a detailed, unemotional response in a declaration that emphasizes the facts.

# Sorry, You Can't Sue the Opposing Attorney

Clients often ask if they can sue the opposing attorney. They can't believe what the attorney has said, done, or threatened. Except in rare cases, people can only sue their own attorney for malpractice. You have no legal standing to sue your opponent's attorney. Malpractice is based on a "duty of care" owed by someone providing a service. Since the opposing attorney is providing a service to your partner, you have no legal standing; only your partner does.

One alternative is to ask the court to sanction the other party's behavior. This includes the attorney's behavior. But courts don't like to attack attorneys, and when they do order sanctions, they order them against the party only. It's up to the other party to sue his own attorney if he believes it was the attorney's fault. Instead of thinking about how outrageous and unfair the other side is, focus on what you can do to improve your case, such as communicating well with your own attorney, gathering factual information, doing research, and choosing your battles.

A week before trial, the attorneys in Sarah's case were required by local rules to "meet and confer," either in person or by phone. "My client doesn't agree with the evaluator's report," said Sam's attorney, "but he might agree with the recommendations, if your client will agree not to pursue child and spousal support."

"That's pretty absurd, and you know it," Sarah's attorney responded. "But I have to tell her about your offer, so I will." He discussed the offer with Sarah, telling her the court would probably order the recommendations and give her some child and spousal support. But, he added, the trial would be costly. In addition, it could be embarrassing and difficult to work with Sam in the future if he lost on everything—and he probably would, since he considered paying support to be so offensive. "Maybe he's a little narcissistic. So you might want to negotiate something with him, however small, to boost his ego," her attorney said.

Sarah decided she needed the child support to help her provide a satisfactory environment for Jay. But she offered to take a small amount of spousal support and limit it to six months while she got herself back to work. After all, Sam wanted to prove that she could make more money, and he might succeed and get an order to pay her no spousal support.

After some heart-to-heart talks with his problem-solving attorney, Sam agreed to Sarah's compromise. Because Sam appeared to have lost interest in her and Jay since his new romance, Sarah didn't think she needed to pursue a restraining order at this time. The case was completely settled and they wouldn't need to go to trial.

Thomas's evaluator could find no evidence consistent with child sexual abuse. In fact, Thomas had volunteered for a lie detector test (which are not admissible in court, but could help with the evaluator) and a psychosexual evaluation on *his own, which indicated he was not being deceptive and didn't have characteristics common to a sex offender.*

*Neither lie detector tests nor psychosexual evaluations are perfect, and the evaluator admitted that no one would ever know with 100 percent certainty whether or not Thomas had molested Brianna. But it appeared so unlikely that the evaluator was willing to make her recommendations. The evaluator had concerns about Tammy's tendency to have "angry outbursts" and a "two-sided" personality: sweet and friendly, then angry and intimidating. The evaluator didn't say "borderline," but the details in the report would support most of the criteria of the diagnosis.*

*The evaluator recommended that Thomas have primary physical custody and Tammy have limited visitation until she completed an anger management class and one year of individual therapy. Tammy refused to accept the report and recommendations. Her attorney said he would fight this "incompetent" evaluation at trial.*

## Conclusion

By now, the blamer's frequent allegations and escalations in court should rarely be surprising to you or your attorney. By working together and anticipating crises, you should be able to respond as strongly and quickly as needed throughout the case. By understanding the dynamics of a negative-advocate attorney, you will spend less time feeling surprised and upset, and more time preparing yourself and responding with accurate information. By understanding the dynamics of a problem-solving attorney, you may be able to settle your case, or at least some issues, out of court. Unfortunately, this is no longer an option for Thomas and many others, so the next chapter focuses on the many predictable problems you may face in court.

*Chapter 13*

# What to Expect at a Hearing or Trial with a Blamer

When you go to family court, forget everything you've seen on television and in the movies. Family courts are crowded, dominated by procedural issues, and unpredictable for the newcomer. The judge has a huge caseload; in family courts they are in the thousands. The judge's preoccupation is moving cases along. The time for hearings is very short and the issues very narrow. Because of the impact of the coronavirus, it may be even harder to get time for court hearings and trials, or there may be long delays.

When blamers are involved, there's a wide range of possible outcomes, from extremely bad to extremely good, but the experience is almost always difficult, especially if you are unprepared. The following explanations emphasize what may go wrong in court. If you're prepared for the realities of these cases, you and your attorney may be able to limit the damage or even prevail.

It helps to think of the court process as having five main "problem areas" of concern when blamers are involved. Each problem area allows the blamer to cause serious problems. But each problem area also allows you an opportunity to assist the court in understanding the blamer's dynamics, clearing yourself of false allegations, and seeking court orders to limit your partner's out-of-control behavior.

**Problem Area 1:** Procedural Manipulations

**Problem Area 2:** Disputes over Evidence

**Problem Area 3:** Troubles with Testimony

**Problem Area 4:** Emotional Persuasion vs. Factual Persuasion

**Problem Area 5:** Obtaining Enforceable Orders

# Overview of Potential Problem Areas

In family court, the judge handles everything, from minor procedural matters to making the big, final decisions. Much of what blamers say in court is inadmissible because it is irrelevant, is unnecessarily inflammatory, or lacks reliability, but this doesn't keep the judge from hearing what they say. Say the blamer's attorney makes an improper statement about you, your attorney makes an objection, and the judge rules on the objection. In reality, it doesn't matter how the judge rules (allowing or disallowing the statement as admissible into evidence); the judge has already heard it! In a civil or criminal case with a jury, if the judge rules the information inadmissible, the jury will never even hear it.

While judges are trained to disregard inadmissible evidence, blamers' highly emotional and dramatic claims grab their attention. Imagine *not* remembering the most horrible information about someone. Also, blamers commonly present so many large and small allegations so quickly that there isn't time or even consciousness of them all enough to object to them all.

# Problem Area 1: Procedural Manipulations

The beginning of most hearings and trials is focused on procedural matters, including the following.

### Giving Proper Notice

Sometimes a blamer or her attorney will improperly give notice for a hearing and then get an order without the other party present. In one case, a blamer without an attorney gave notice of an "emergency" hearing to the target's probation officer, who was not in daily contact with the target. The next day the blamer lied to the court about giving proper notice and obtained a substantial amount of the target's reserved funds in court, based on completely false statements (the target wasn't there to refute them). The order was eventually set aside but at great expense.

Here's another example: An attorney gave notice of an emergency hearing by mailing papers to the target's attorney after the hearing. The target's attorney immediately went to court, and the orders were "vacated" (set aside).

While these examples are rare, they happen when a highly manipulative blamer or negative-advocate attorney is involved. To be safe, check your file at court from time to time to see whether anything you don't know about has been added or decided without you.

### Continuances

Most courts will grant at least one continuance (the postponing of a court hearing to a later date) of almost any matter at the request of either party. This allows time for a party to get an attorney, obtain more useful information for the court to consider, or respond to new events.

Blamers want to be in control of as many issues as possible, including minor events and information. If you are ready and eager to get the case going at court, the blamer will ask for one or more continuances at the last minute, after you have gone to great lengths to be fully prepared. But if you need more time, the blamer may try to force the case to go forward immediately, arguing against a reasonable continuance.

When there are agreements for continuances by both sides, they can be phoned in to the court or submitted in written stipulations so that no one has to go to court and waste time. But blamers go to court even for continuances, making additional attorney fees necessary and requiring you to miss work. There may be court rules requiring or disallowing continuances in certain circumstances, yet the blamer will still try to get around them. Discuss the likelihood of continuances with your attorney and become familiar with the court rules in your county. Missed work and attorney fees are part of the court process, especially when blamers are involved. The more flexible you are, the better you may be able to cope.

Remember, you're in this for the long run. Don't let yourself get too frustrated by petty manipulations around these minor procedural issues. Your focus should always be on preparing for the opportunity to present full and accurate information. If you have to wait another month to do so because of a continuance you didn't want, spend it gathering even more useful information.

### Document Deadlines

Each court may have its own deadlines for the submission of documents prior to a hearing or trial. Make sure you've discussed the local rules with your attorney so you can get documents to her with plenty of time to make the deadlines. It isn't unusual for blamers and their negative-advocate attorneys to try to manipulate these deadlines. They may submit declarations to court late but claim that the information is very important and must be considered. You may be caught with little time to respond or be unable to respond, in which case you might be able to get the court to disallow the late declaration.

The judge has discretion to either grant a continuance to allow you time to respond or decide to consider it anyway. It may be best to quickly prepare a response to the late declaration and submit it to the court. If the judge decides to consider the late declaration, the court will probably consider your response as well.

With certain attorneys, you can almost predict that they will submit documents late, even the day of the hearing or trial. In that case, bring a declaration with responses in anticipation of the late information.

## Problem Area 2: Disputes over Evidence

Blamers will try to get information into evidence that is irrelevant, improperly acquired, unreliable, and peripheral to your case. At the same time, they will object to your evidence— especially the most accurate information about the blamer's private behavior. This battle over evidence becomes a large part of the game of court. Yet it is extremely serious, because courts can be swayed by the peripheral emotional persuasion of much of the blamer's evidence. There is always the risk that the judge will deny some or all of your own best evidence.

### Documents

There are many rules about documents, declarations, depositions, and testimony. Simply keeping track of the deadlines for each type of evidence can be a full-time job. If you miss a deadline, it can completely rule out some of your evidence. Demands for information, subpoenas, interrogatories, and depositions must all be finished well before a court date. There may be a cutoff date of thirty days or more before trial, depending on your state and county rules.

Blamers may violate or try to violate many of these rules. Then they will beg you and your attorney to grant an extension for submitting evidence. The court encourages cooperation between the parties and their attorneys, so you're expected to agree to "reasonable" requests. Of course, blamers push the limits of "reasonable" far beyond what most people would do. You may constantly be facing decisions about the amount of flexibility you'll allow the other party.

Follow your attorney's advice about this. Otherwise, you may be targeted as the unreasonable person in court if you always say no. At the same time, blamers and their attorneys may try to hold you to the absolute letter of the law regarding these same cutoff dates and rules of evidence. They may make a very big deal of something very small. In one case, a blamer's attorney had made several requests for extensions and changes regarding a trial. The target's attorney consented. Then, when it came time for trial exhibits to be exchanged three days before the trial, a major problem arose for the target's attorney, who requested an extension from 5:00 p.m. to the next morning at 9:00 a.m. The blamer's attorney returned the call in the afternoon and refused the extension. The target's exhibits were rushed to the blamer's attorney and arrived at 5:05 p.m. At the beginning of the trial, the blamer's attorney made a motion objecting to all fifty of the target's exhibits, because they were five minutes "late." The target's attorney described the prior agreed-on extensions for the other side, and the judge accepted the target's trial exhibits.

Unless there is an agreement regarding the admission of documents as evidence, they must be authenticated by someone testifying as a witness: "Ms. Jones, do you recognize this document? How did you receive this document?" This can be a slow process, but officially it is necessary and a common area of dispute in high-conflict cases. Blamers want to argue about very minor details while avoiding the bigger issues. Be prepared to let go of a minor document or two, in order to get the most important ones into evidence.

## Problem Area 3: Troubles with Testimony

Testimony is one of the primary, and most dramatic, forms of evidence presented in court. While many family courts prefer written declarations as the main form of evidence (they are usually quicker to read and more to the point), oral testimony is also a common option. You should discuss with your attorney whether you should testify in court as a witness in your own case. Also, find out whether you need to have a written declaration on file in order to testify, which may be required for some hearings but not others. These rules are very important and should be available at your court clerk's office.

The testimony of professionals is often the most persuasive with the court, because the judge considers them to provide a neutral analysis and explanation of the case, especially regarding issues that are beyond the judge's own areas of expertise. But even professionals make mistakes. If you have an evaluator who was emotionally hooked by the blamer and has jumped to inaccurate conclusions, then have another professional testify to show the weaknesses of the evaluator's report. Or cross-examine the evaluator to emphasize the weaknesses in his methods or analysis.

Witnesses in general should testify only if they are credible and can provide relevant information to the issues and decisions before the court. "Character witnesses" are usually not wanted by the court. Everyone can get someone to say something nice about them. It still may be beneficial to have family or friends testify as witnesses about their specific observations if they directly relate to the issues before the court. If there is conflicting information, the judge will get a clearer idea of which witness is credible and which is not. In a case involving a family business and substantial family loans, a blamer with NPD made up many false, but believable, "emotional facts." After relatives on each side testified about the actual facts of the family loans, it was obvious whose story held together and whose didn't.

But witnesses can present many unknowns. It's best for your attorney to depose important witnesses before the trial, to see how they will behave and to get an idea of their testimonies. Also, using the transcript of the deposition at trial can prove very helpful at catching contradictions between stories made up by a chronically lying blamer.

It may or may not be helpful to your case if the blamer testifies. In many cases, it's better not to call the blamer as a witness. New allegations commonly occur that raise new suspicions about you with no time to challenge them. Blamers are too unpredictable and can appear quite credible. Bonding with and lying to people in authority are their strengths. Also, if they testify first, they may create a good "first impression" that sticks with the court. Bill prefers to call his own client as a witness to tell the accurate story first, if he can (who goes first depends on state and county rules).

### Cross-Examination of a Blamer

Cross-examination occurs after the opposing attorney has asked a witness general questions. Then your attorney can ask very specific questions to challenge the witness's memory and credibility. (This will also happen if you testify.) Help your attorney know what questions may reveal lies and contradictory statements. This doesn't have to be a dramatic process, but it might be. This is where the art of cross-examination may make a difference.

You may be tempted to have your lawyer aggressively confront the blamer to expose his private persona that is usually hidden. How to handle this witness is a judgment call for your attorney. If the blamer is easily angered, you may be tempted to have your attorney confront the person to get an angry explosion, as they do in the movies and on TV, but the other side may object to this approach as "badgering the witness," or the judge may be turned off by this aggressive manner.

Judges prefer that attorneys ask questions of the parties in a professional and respectful manner. Therefore, try to get the blamer to make certain statements that later are shown to be false or contradictory. Most of the time, you're more likely to catch a blamer with other evidence of false statements and misbehavior, rather than a revealing emotional explosion in the courtroom.

At trial, it is more persuasive to look like the reasonable side. You will have time to bring out the contradictions in the blamer's testimony and evidence. Avoid dramatic and unpredictable confrontations. Remember, you're in court because you cannot control the blamer's behavior. Do not assume you'll control the blamer just because she's on the witness stand.

Research the blamer's prior statements and documents, then provide questions to your attorney, so she can thoroughly question the blamer about his actions and evidence. Bring out the blamer's inconsistencies, but don't allow time for him to create "cover stories" to credibly explain his glaring contradictions. Blamers are particularly skilled at this. If they know where you're going, they will make up credible-sounding stories.

It may be more effective to get the blamer to become committed to her false statements on the witness stand. Then, after she's done as a witness, have your attorney point out the true, verifiable information that shows she's making false statements—either with another witness or by lining up the contradictory evidence during the closing argument, when it's too late for another "cover story."

## Should You Testify?

This is also a judgment call you should discuss at length with your attorney. In some cases, you may be your own worst enemy and should not testify. In other cases, your reasonable manner and consistent explanations may help the judge trust you and disbelieve the other side. If you testify, the blamer's attorney will try to make you look bad—and try to get you to have an angry explosion like in the movies or on TV. If you're properly prepared for this (you may want to practice with your attorney), your reasonable responses will make the opposing attorney look bad for harassing you, and you'll look good.

Remember, many attorneys believe everything their blamer clients tell them. They are quite surprised when the target doesn't respond in an uncontrollable rage as they were told to expect.

## Problem Area 4: Emotional Persuasion vs. Factual Persuasion

As we have mentioned throughout this book, emotional persuasion is one of the biggest problems in court with a blamer. In general, the shorter the hearing, the higher the risk that the judge will make negative orders based on the blamer's emotional persuasion. The judge is not an investigator, but a decision maker. The burden is on the parties and their counsel to gather information and persuade the court. (Remember the charts in the middle of chapter 6, which show emotional persuasion versus fact finding. This tension often continues throughout a case, at every hearing.)

Longer hearings and a trial give you the opportunity to present facts and explain patterns of the blamer's bad behavior and false statements in depth. When there's a choice, you will be better off seeking a longer hearing or a trial, so you can present the facts and help the judge see the unchanging pattern of harmful behavior, rather than view an event as an isolated incident "caused" by the divorce. The burden is on you to make your presentation move quickly and focus on this pattern, so that the court will recognize the need for court intervention to stop the pattern.

In the early stages of the court process (at emergency "protective" hearings or minor motions before the court), there may not be time to explain that, rather than being accurate statements, much of the blamer's statements are about "emotional facts," which spring from her cognitive distortions. In the absence of good evidence to the contrary, the court will be persuaded to take a "cautious" approach and make whatever orders the blamer requests.

With a longer hearing or trial, factual persuasion will hopefully show the court that the emotional persuasion was based on false or misleading information. Factual persuasion comes from documents, declarations by neutral third parties (who know both sides, or who are professionals involved with one or both parties), and court-appointed evaluators.

After the factual persuasion process has given the court a more accurate picture, the blamer's emotions may be less persuasive. But this part of the process significantly depends on your willingness to gather and bring forward factual information that may be quite harmful to the blamer. It may make the blamer angry, and he may threaten you. Be prepared for the blamer to escalate the case at this point by attacking you physically, verbally, or with new legal procedures.

The blamer may try to go to another court, where this information isn't yet known. She may make up more and more dramatic and false claims against you, in hopes of regaining the upper hand and capturing the attention of the judge, yet again, to her side of the case. She will try to gather new negative advocates to make claims against you and to argue for her anew. In many cases, the court makes all its decisions while in the emotional persuasion phase of the case. Try to get enough time to thoroughly present accurate information to the court by asking for longer hearings. Even if there are some bad temporary decisions, try to schedule later hearings, where more-complete information may come out.

## Problem Area 5: Obtaining Enforceable Orders

Suppose all goes surprisingly well and you "win" your case, clear your name, and get a decision based on facts, not emotional persuasion. Your judge may make orders about the blamer's behavior, parenting plan, support payments, property division, and sometimes attorney fees.

All of these orders may be useless with a partner who has BP, NP, or ASP traits and is still blaming.

People with BP traits sometimes refuse to follow court orders because they feel "abandoned" by the court (now they blame the judge). Instead, they focus their energy on new hearings, gathering new negative advocates and possibly a new judge in an effort to prove that their cognitive distortions were correct all along. People with narcissistic traits feel demeaned and usually have disdain for the court's orders (they, too, blame the judge). To follow the orders would make them less than the "superior" people they believe they are.

So you'll need to get really strong court orders that are very detailed, including clear-cut terms for actions to be taken: who does what, when, and how. The orders will need to have precise consequences for noncompliance and as few loopholes as possible. Blamers are known for finding even the smallest exception to the rules and orders, and they focus on those loopholes as justification for their noncompliance.

Of course, some negative-advocate attorneys will help them do this. After all, attorneys are trained to find exceptions to the rules to help their clients, but their success helps their clients stay stuck in their cognitive distortions rather than get help, much as attorneys for drunk drivers used to help them keep driving without really getting sober.

Enforcing the orders will be up to you and your attorney. If money is involved, you may need to put restraints on accounts. If there's a parenting plan, you may need to keep a journal of noncompliance. If there are restraining orders, you may need to be prepared to call the police to enforce them, if the blamer contacts you improperly.

Do not undermine the court's orders in any way; otherwise, the blamer will be able to neutralize your later complaints. A woman who obtained a restraining order decided to make a quick call to her former boyfriend, despite the restraining order against his calling her. They had a nice chat and then started calling each other—despite the restraining order. Then he started coming over. One day she didn't want him to come over, but he came anyway. She called the police. At court, the boyfriend was able to prove that she had been calling him. This almost caused the termination of the restraining order.

*Tammy's attorney called the psychological evaluator as a witness. The attorney was very aggressive with the evaluator, first challenging her credentials. But the judge quickly accepted her as a witness, because she had qualified before at several hearings and trials with this judge. She met the training requirements for custody evaluators and had over a dozen years of experience performing evaluations.*

"*What is the child's date of birth?*" Tammy's attorney asked.

The evaluator replied, "*She's four years old; I don't remember the exact date.*"

"*Well, you got it wrong in your report. Look at page 7,*" he said accusingly. "*If you got such a basic fact wrong, what else did you get wrong?*"

Thomas's attorney said, "*Objection: argumentative.*" The court sustained the objection, and Tammy's attorney went on to ask a different question. After an hour, it was Thomas's attorney's turn to ask the evaluator questions. After some introductory questions, he asked, "*Do your findings support a diagnosis of borderline personality disorder?*"

"*Objection: argumentative!*" exclaimed Tammy's attorney. The judge sustained the objection, saying, "*I don't wish to get into a discussion of each party's personality. I don't think it would be productive. I want to focus on the specific problems, and I especially want to hear discussion of what orders will help here. Do you want my tentative opinion at this point, or do you wish to go further with testimony?*"

After conferring with their clients, both attorneys asked for the judge's "*tentative opinion.*"

"*I think Dr. Harbert did an excellent and thorough job evaluating this family. I agree with her recommendations, except I am going to give the mother a little more visitation time than recommended if she assures me I won't hear about any problems with her visitation.*

"*I don't want either of you discussing this case with the child. If there are to be reports of abuse, they are to be made to Child Protective Services, not in ex parte hearings unless the authorities say so.*

"*I don't find any credible evidence that Thomas molested the child. I also don't find any credible evidence that Tammy knowingly made false allegations, but these findings could change with more testimony. I am concerned about some of the behavior patterns here."*

*The attorneys met with their clients, and both agreed to accept the judge's tentative decision as the orders of the court.*

*Tammy's lawyer told her she was better off not risking getting less time with Brianna and a finding that she knowingly lied. If the court made that determination, Tammy could be liable for all of Thomas's attorney fees, as he had requested.*

*Thomas knew that by accepting the judge's tentative decision, he would lose out on the chance of getting attorney fees. But Tammy might be more cooperative by accepting the court's tentative opinion, as the judge seemed to imply.*

# What If You Are Losing Your Case?

Despite your best efforts, sometimes blamers are highly successful and the judge gets the case backward: gives custody to the more dysfunctional parent, restricts the healthier parent's visitation rights, issues restraining orders against innocent parties, and financially rewards people who make false statements and mismanage funds. Unfortunately, that's why we call this type of partner a persuasive blamer. They are skilled at covering up their disorders and preoccupied with attacking those close to them. Ironically, in the adversarial process of court, these personality characteristics can be very persuasive.

Keep in mind that judges don't make bad decisions on purpose. It's usually the result of insufficient information before the court, the court's general lack of knowledge about underlying PDs and traits, or both. It also may not be at all personal, because in many cases, the judge's hands are tied and she has to make certain orders. There are several issues to consider.

## Are You Really Losing?

In many cases, frustrated parties feel that they are losing when they've actually obtained the best possible result under the circumstances. There are many public policies that affect the courts in seemingly unpredictable ways. For example, a husband was always very responsible about sending his child-support and spousal-support checks to his former wife. Yet when he went to court and won a reduction in support payments because of changed circumstances, the court ordered for his employer to deduct the payments from his paychecks. While he felt he had lost because this made him look bad to his employer, it's public policy to require "wage garnishment" orders to enforce support whenever the decision is made, regardless of the specific case history.

Here's another example: A father who was convicted of child abuse was allowed to have supervised visitation, when the mother thought there should have been a permanent no-contact order. The reason is that public policy encourages frequent contact with both parents, regardless of what they have done, as long as the child is protected.

## Are You Being Assertive Enough?

At the beginning of this book, we talked about the need to use an assertive approach when dealing with a partner with BP, NP, or ASP traits. When cases go badly, sometimes it's because you are being too aggressive or too passive. Perhaps you have engaged in some aggressive acts yourself and not realized how that can hurt you in court (such as angry confrontations during child exchanges). Perhaps you have held back on important information that might make a difference to the judge. Perhaps you have given in to the blamer too often, which has encouraged her to keep fighting you. It may be that you need to practice more assertiveness skills, which you can discuss with your therapist. It often helps to practice or role-play situations, so that you get used to speaking up more often and in a very reasonable manner.

## Get a Second Opinion

You can always get another opinion from another attorney or expert. You're not obliged to tell your current attorney or expert that you're doing this. The second opinion may actually be that you're doing as well as you can under the limitations of the law or the facts of your specific case. There's no need to alienate your present attorney or expert by telling him about this, since you might decide to keep using his services.

It often helps to get a fresh explanation of court procedures, local court culture, and public policies. A specialist or an expert in a particular subject may point out new laws. A brief consultation with someone else may give you new ideas for gathering information or making new arguments in court. Ask the new expert whether she thinks making a change is beneficial. It looks bad to change attorneys a lot, so make sure this is a necessary move.

## Changing Attorneys

Some attorneys don't have the skills, knowledge, attitude, or time to truly help you in your case. It may be very difficult for you to know this in advance, despite your research. Sometimes circumstances change once your case gets going. With a blamer on the other side, your case is very likely to quickly escalate at the beginning and remain high conflict and unresolved for a long time.

Cases involving partners with BP, NP, or ASP traits can be frustrating and disruptive to your attorney's schedule. Your partner's negative-advocate attorney may harass your attorney with unnecessary hearings, correspondence, demands for discovery, and personal attacks. Your attorney may not have the emotional stamina or simply not want this kind of case. That's why we said earlier that you must discuss these issues before retaining someone, and make sure you pay your attorney on time so she doesn't waver in her commitment when the going gets rough.

If you're thinking about switching attorneys, do it when there's enough time for the new attorney to get up to speed in your case. Don't wait until the week before trial. The judge may not give you a continuance (more time). Also, retain a new attorney before terminating your current one so that you're always covered in case of an unexpected accusation or legal hassle from your soon-to-be ex. Be certain that a change is necessary before you switch. Do your homework and hire someone you can work with through thick and thin. It can hurt your credibility in court to go through lots of attorneys, but in a complex or high-conflict case, it's not unusual to have at least one change.

If you do change attorneys, prepare yourself for a different approach, share your concerns, and ask how you can be most helpful. The new attorney can get your file and notify the old attorney of the change. It's up to you if you want to clear the air with your old attorney. Sometimes it helps to have your old attorney as an ally if you need information or friendly assistance later on. Don't burn any bridges.

## Conclusion

There are many predictable opportunities for a BP, NP, or ASP blamer to manipulate the family court process, often in an effort to keep a sense of power and control over the blamer's own chaotic life and your life. Courts are not designed to recognize the blamer's deceptions and cognitive distortions, which often play out in unnecessary, but predictable, arguments over court procedures and evidence.

But court hearings or a trial may give you the opportunity to explain patterns of the blamer's unchanging harmful behavior, false statements, and the need for court intervention. With careful preparation, you and your lawyer may be able to overcome a persuasive blamer's emotional persuasion with factual persuasion. You may be successful, and the judge may make favorable court orders. Be careful to make sure the orders are specific enough to be enforceable when your partner with BP, NP, or ASP traits may feel abandoned or insulted and try to avoid following them.

Judges have limitations on the decisions they can make, and you may feel frustrated with the court process even though you were as successful as possible. You also may feel frustrated with your attorney. Get a second opinion before making any big changes. If you do decide to change attorneys, try not to do this too often.

In some cases, once the other side realizes you're being highly assertive in bringing accurate information to court and countering their false information, they will back down and consider settling the case. In other cases, alternatives to litigation may be possible from the start. In part 3 we will look at those options and help you weigh when they may be appropriate for you, now that you know something about the realities of family court.

*Chapter 14*

# Presenting Your Case

When you are dealing with a partner with borderline, narcissistic, or antisocial personality disorder or traits, it's important
to know that you can't successfully use those labels in court.
A judge will be turned off immediately unless there has been
a formal diagnosis by a mental health professional that the
partner does not challenge. This is rare. More often you can
see their personality patterns, your lawyer can see them and
other people can, but it is not official. Yet there is a way to
deal with this.

Whether you have a lawyer or are representing yourself, you
can present your ex-partner's troublesome behavior patterns to
evaluators and the judge using the following approaches.

## Present the Three Theories of the High-Conflict Case

To avoid getting stuck with any unspoken presumptions by the
decision maker (see chapter 6), you might say something like
the following:

I understand that there are three theories to consider in any case where one person says that the other is acting badly. These all look alike on the surface:

1. Person B says Person A is acting badly and it's true.

2. Person B says Person A is acting badly, but it's not at all true and person B is acting badly and possibly projecting their issues onto person A.

3. Person B and Person A are both acting badly.

In this case, I am saying that _____ is acting badly by engaging in _____ abusive behavior and my evidence will show this. (Theory 1)

Or:

In this case, _____ is saying that I am acting badly, but I am not. These allegations are false. Instead, _____ is acting badly by making these false statements and acting badly in other ways, which my evidence will show. (Theory 2)

By saying this to any decision maker (evaluator, judge, or other), you are putting your case into a proper perspective and discouraging them from jumping to conclusions that fit their presumption, if they have one. You also make their job easier, as you are giving them exactly the type of information they need to make their difficult decisions.

# Document Three or Four Patterns of Concerning Behavior

Evaluators and judges have dozens and sometimes hundreds of cases that they are handling at the same time as yours. They have a lot of information in common, so that your case needs to be made simple and memorable. Rather than describing the history of your case chronologically in great detail, you need to get their attention by presenting the three or four most concerning patterns of behavior of the BP, NP, or ASP right away, so that they know what category to put your case into in their minds.

In particular, some evaluators and many judges try to treat most of their cases as if both parties are acting equally badly (Theory 3) and therefore they give them a cookie-cutter set of court orders: both shouldn't make disparaging remarks in front of the children, both should get substantial parenting time, both should take a parenting class, and so forth, regardless of the history. But if the other person has a personality disorder or traits, you need to explain how your case is different, without saying that they have a personality disorder. For example: "In this case, [Mr. or Ms.] Smith has a pattern of *violence toward the children*, a pattern of *undermining my relationship* with the children, and a pattern of *making false statements*."

If you are submitting written information, then use headings such as these phrases in bold to make it easy for the decision maker to absorb what you are saying. It also helps to refer back to these themes several times during your presentation, either in writing or verbally, so that they will be remembered.

Then, give three of the most extreme behaviors under each of your headings, such as in the following example.

# Violence Toward the Children

1. On May 1, _____ slammed the door on our son's hand out of anger.

2. On June 3, _____ grabbed our daughter's arm, claiming she wasn't listening, and gave her a bruise.

3. On June 4, _____ tore the shirt partly off our son in anger when he didn't get into the car fast enough in the parking lot by a store. A witness saw this and called the police. The report is attached.

# Undermining My Relationship

1. On April 14, _____ scheduled an all-day Saturday visit with her out-of-town parents and our son during my parenting time, without contacting me or getting my permission. It ruined my weekend with our son as I was going to take him and a friend fishing that day. I only had a half day Sunday, before he went back for the week with the other parent.

2. On May 11, _____ yelled at me in front of the children during a parenting exchange, saying that I owed money to the dentist. This was not at all true, as I had paid my half and the dentist was waiting for _____ to pay the other half. This is a common event during our exchanges.

3. On numerous occasions, the children have told me that _____ says I am the cause of the divorce and they have questioned me about whether I was having an affair, whether I was using drugs, and whether I was threatening to quit my job.

# Making False Statements

1. On June 1, I got a call from Child Protective Services saying that someone said our son was being abused in my home, so they wanted to come out and meet with me. They did an investigation and determined that the report was unfounded. _____ later admitted that he/she had called in the report.

2. On June 4, _____ took our son to a counselor and said that my new partner was abusing the boy and that life in my house "was a living hell." The counselor wanted to talk to me, but _____ lied and said I was out of town and unavailable. It's easy to prove that I was in town and could have been easily reached by phone. When I finally found out and spoke to the counselor, the counselor was already angry with me based on _____'s false statements.

3. On June 15, _____ told the court that his/her income was only $800 per month. But the payroll records I received show he/she was actually receiving $2,000 per month at that time. See the attached transcript and payroll records.

Very quickly the reader will get a picture of what is going on. But it's very important not to exaggerate or you will lose credibility. Facts matter. If your themes do not match the facts, then you will be considered overdramatic or even lying yourself. Other important information may be doubted. For example, in your case there may be no violence toward the children. In that case, find other more accurate themes to present, such as *mood swings and anger*, or *lack of empathy for children*, or *undermining of doctor's orders*, or *yelling at children*, or *lying to the court*. Whatever the three or four most concerning behaviors, this information can help the judge understand how your case is different from two ordinary parents arguing.

This can also help your judge see how clear you are in communicating your realistic concerns. If your partner is like many high-conflict people in family court, he or she will ramble on with blame about so many problems that it will be hard for the decision maker to focus clearly on their biggest concerns.

While you aren't giving the decision makers a diagnosis of your partner, you are showing how these patterns of behavior may more or less fit the patterns of a personality disorder. For example, BPs often show extreme mood swings, intense anger, and manipulation of professionals. NPs often show lack of empathy, disinterest in the child's needs, and undermining of the other parent. ASPs often show lying to professionals, teaching antisocial behavior, and violating the law (like driving the children without seat belts or getting speeding tickets). But the patterns of concerning behavior in your case may not fit any particular personality disorder, which is fine. Any patterns of concerning behavior give a much clearer picture of your partner than any diagnosis could.

Also, make sure that the patterns that you present are related to the decisions you are requesting. For example, if your partner lied on his or her tax returns, this won't help you show that they shouldn't have more parenting time, but it may help you show that their income statements are likely to be false for calculating child support.

These are just examples and should not be used in your case unless they really fit. Using this approach, you have a better chance of getting the evaluator or judge's attention focused on the true nature of your case.

Sometimes it even helps to say something like this: "I understand that in a normal case the other parent would have substantial or equal parenting time, and I wish that could be true in our case. However, the [father/mother] has such a severe pattern of behavior that there should be limited parenting time to protect our son and daughter, for the reasons that I will describe." This shows that you realize how your case is not a usual case, but that you are a reasonable person who understands and respects the normal approaches for normal cases.

## Explain Your Request for Orders

Whether you are presenting your information to an evaluator or the judge, make your request for orders fit the problems that you have described. Sadly, some evaluators and many judges will still be inclined to make normal court orders even after hearing how abnormal your case is. They may simply admonish the other person to follow the court order, act reasonably, and stop doing the bad behavior they were doing. But some evaluators and many judges still don't understand that personality disorders really are *enduring patterns* of behavior and that they won't be changing any time soon, if ever, regardless of the harsh or sensitive lecture the judge gives them. Here is an example of what you or your lawyer might say when requesting court orders:

> Your honor, these patterns have repeated and repeated and repeated for so long that they are not going to change, even with a lecture from the court or admonishment from any other professional. We have shown the sad history here and seen that lectures don't work. This is the nature of _____'s problems. Therefore, we are requesting strong court orders to protect the children and myself. If _____ changes in the future, that's great. But court orders should not be based on that extremely unlikely outcome unless it has already happened.

# Conclusion

With this overall approach, you are more likely to be viewed favorably by the court. This is especially important if you have been losing your case and not getting the full picture to the decision makers. Remember that people with PDs can be very emotionally persuasive, but they are usually not well organized and focused, although their lawyers may be. By giving simple, repetitive, theme-organized important information to the decision makers, you make their jobs easier and they are more likely to grasp the severity of your case.

PART 3

# Succeeding
# Out of Court

Chapter 15

# Considering Alternatives to Litigation with a Blamer

*Before he told Tammy he wanted a divorce, Thomas hired an attorney, and they discussed his options. His attorney said, "Mediation might be the place to start, if you think she can sit in the same room with you and a neutral mediator and reasonably discuss all of the issues of the divorce. I don't have to be there. It will save you money. I can discuss the case along the way and review your written marital settlement agreement before you sign it.*

*"Of course, from your description of her, she may not be able to handle that. So another alternative is for you, me, her, and her attorney to meet together in a four-way conference. We can discuss the issues together with the opportunity for both of you to take breaks and meet separately with your attorneys. A new approach that expands on this idea is collaborative divorce, with two attorneys, one or two mental health coaches, a financial specialist, and a child specialist. Each professional helps manage the process while helping you make decisions out of court. But these methods include face-to-face meetings, so it's hard to predict whether Tammy can*

*be productive in these settings. Sometimes they help someone like her maintain self-control, and other times they cause the person to lose it.*

*"Often, in cases like yours, it's best to have each of your attorneys just talk to each other by phone, send proposal letters back and forth, and meet separately with their clients. This reduces the emotional contact and allows each of you to have a special relationship with your attorney, so that someone can discuss the legal standards with Tammy outside your presence and calmly discuss compromises she may not want to make.*

*"Keep in mind that it takes both of you to agree to negotiate out of court. If she just wants to go to court and fight, then that's where we'll end up, and we should always prepare for that possibility."*

After considering today's court culture, many reasonable people prefer to settle their divorces out of court. The vast majority of couples never have a court hearing. Their terms of settlement, commonly called a *stipulation* or *marital settlement agreement* (depending on your state), are then filed with the court and become the orders of the court concerning the terms of the parenting agreement or divorce.

Judges, therapists, and most attorneys encourage the parties to attempt an out-of-court settlement, primarily because:

- Agreements generate less animosity.

- The costs are much less.

- Agreements are just as enforceable as a judge's orders when filed with the court.

- Agreements are actually followed more often by those who participate in making them than orders imposed by a judge.

Considering alternatives to litigation is so important that we made this part of our acronym KEEP CALM. You don't give up any rights by attempting to settle the issues through one or more alternative methods. The decision to use an alternative to court must be made jointly by the parties, which often appears unlikely when a blamer is involved. (An exception to this is court-mandated alternatives, such as with some court-based custody and visitation mediators, described next.) Some partners with BP, NP, or ASP traits are able to resolve their parenting issues or divorces mostly out of court, if they have skillful assistance in shifting from blame to compromise. (See the chart titled "Three Divorce Scenarios" in chapter 5.) You should make the decision to use one of the following methods in consultation with your attorney and therapist.

# Self-Directed Negotiations

In most states, the parties are encouraged to negotiate and draft a divorce settlement agreement out of court, but it must meet court requirements, which are sometimes quite complicated. Although many people try this on their own, we advise getting professional assistance, especially when a blamer is involved.

One of the risks of negotiating for yourself is that you may inadvertently give up legal rights (to alimony, interest in retirement plans, stock options, custody and visitation modifications, and so on) that are very hard to get back. When you're negotiating with a blamer, he will pressure you to give him much more than a court would provide, because of his cognitive distortions that he deserves more because he was "abandoned" or is "superior."

# Divorce Mediation

The courts increasingly encourage mediation, which helps parties save money and (perhaps) remain on civil terms with each other, especially for the sake of the children. Mediation also keeps the decision making in the parties' hands and can result in more detailed agreements. It's usually confidential and has no impact on the court if there is no agreement. Therefore, it's usually a risk-free process. With the lasting impact of the coronavirus, mediation has become more popular because it is easier and quicker to get into than the courthouse.

In mediation, the parties meet together (with some exceptions, described next) with one neutral mediator, who informs and educates them (but doesn't give legal advice), guides them in making proposals, and facilitates reaching agreement on the issues. The mediator is not allowed to take sides and does not make the decisions (although some make recommendations, as described next). Attorneys usually don't attend mediation sessions, but parties may consult with their attorneys between sessions and have their attorneys write up or review the final court papers.

An attorney-mediator can provide some general information (but not advice) to both of you, so that the blamer understands the standards, options, costs, and consequences of going to court over any particular issue, presented by a neutral person. Sometimes it helps to have a reasonable support person there during the mediation for one or both parties, because this person can reassure an anxious partner with BP, NP, or ASP traits and can suggest breaks to allow time for the support person to privately explain the advantages of settlement to your partner. Of course, this fails if the support person gets too emotionally involved, so be careful about who you agree will attend.

It helps to ask yourself whether you believe your blamer can sit in the same room with you and listen quietly to statements and proposals she disagrees with. Mild blamers and some moderate blamers can handle this, with enough structure and direction. Some mediators shuttle back and forth between the parties in separate rooms. Others may do most of the mediation over the phone with the parties at separate locations or make separate calls back and forth between the parties. Make sure your mediator is experienced and can give you some success stories if he uses an unusual approach.

Mediation is less likely to be successful with severe blamers for several reasons: their all-or-nothing thinking often prevents compromises, they cannot listen to ideas that conflict with their reality, the abandonment feels too intense to them, and they cannot handle the combination of physical closeness and emotional distance (ending the relationship while still sitting together in the same room).

## Choosing a Divorce Mediator

It's not uncommon for couples to interview three mediators before selecting one. It's best to get a recommendation from people who know the mediator's work. But large organizations like the Academy of Professional Family Mediators have lists of mediators by geographic areas. You both need to feel comfortable with the mediator, but watch out for mediators with very little mediation experience. They can get emotionally "hooked" and take sides, rather than stay neutral, when a blamer is involved.

## Court-Required Child Mediation

Many states require mediation prior to a hearing on any disputes about child custody or visitation, but not usually for financial issues. Typically there is just one meeting with the court-related mediator of approximately one to two hours. Mild blamers and some moderate blamers may be able to reach an agreement, but severe blamers have a difficult time agreeing to anything and usually go to court to fight—even when it appears likely that they will lose.

In some jurisdictions, mediators write a report and recommendation to the judge if there is no agreement. This is called *nonconfidential mediation*. You should ask whether a written recommendation is the procedure for your court's mediators. If so, you should be totally prepared for this process, similar to preparing for any evaluator, as described in chapter 11.

## Mediation and Domestic Violence

If there are allegations of domestic violence, the parties can usually ask to be seen separately. Seeing the mediator separately may or may not make an agreement more likely, depending on the mediator's skills. Requesting to be seen separately has its pros and cons. If you're the victim of physical or severe emotional abuse, doing so may be necessary for you to feel safe. But in mild and moderate cases, it's often better to be in the room with your blamer and the mediator, so that you know what the blamer is saying about you. Then you can respond with more accurate information during the same meeting and avoid allowing the blamer's emotions to sway the mediator.

## Collaborative Divorce

In collaborative divorce, there's a team of two lawyers and possibly one or two mental health coaches, a financial specialist, and a child specialist, if there are children. The professionals are required to sign an agreement that they will withdraw from the case if a settlement is not reached and it goes to court, which creates a powerful incentive to settle the case out of court.

This approach is becoming more popular in general and has the potential to help manage blamers, because there is a team of professionals on their "side" while the goal is a negotiated settlement. Some moderate and many severe blamers often force issues into court anyway—to avoid acceptance or compromise. As with mediation, it may be worth it to see whether a collaborative team can help contain the conflict with your partner enough to reach a full settlement without going to court.

Collaborative divorce may appear expensive, with all of the professionals involved. But it's often less expensive than most court cases with a blamer, because the collaborative process discourages "splitting," whereas the court process reinforces it. In collaborative divorce, there is no place for accusatory declarations, surprise hearings, or surprise discovery demands.

## Negotiations with Attorneys

**Negotiate out of court.** If collaborative divorce does not work in your case, we encourage you to obtain a problem-solving attorney, as described in chapter 12, who will be able to take your case to court but will still make efforts to negotiate out of court as much as possible. Typically, attorney negotiations involve a series of phone calls and letters that resolve the issues, and the parties never need to talk directly to each other unless they want to. Having the attorneys act as buffers helps keep things calm and controlled, which is especially important when a blamer is involved. Then, if there are any unresolved issues, the attorney is already familiar with your case and ready to go to court.

Keep in mind that it's not uncommon for blamers to fire a negotiating attorney because they don't like keeping the issues narrow and being calmed down when they are upset. Some just want to fight. In this case, they often hire an attorney who will take many of the issues to court instead. A blamer who fires a reasonable negotiating attorney commonly seeks a negative-advocate attorney, which was discussed in chapter 12.

**Negotiate at court.** Many negotiations also occur in the hallways of the court building, just before a scheduled court hearing, which often involves the attorneys talking to each other and then going back and forth between clients who are sitting far apart, especially if they are not on speaking terms. When blamers are involved, their level of tension may be so high just from being in the court building that they are unable to meaningfully negotiate. Some other blamers respond only to the pressure of being in court and having a decision hanging over their heads; then they settle in the hallway right before the hearing rather than risk humiliation in the courtroom.

Bill recommends trying to start by negotiating away from the courthouse when blamers are involved, because they often need time and physical space to back off and settle down. When they are at court, many are unable to do this and feel backed into a corner. They may impulsively risk the court battle in an effort to save face, and end up with a much worse result.

But if the blamer and her attorney insist on having all decisions made at the courthouse, then don't try to talk them out of it. It may make you appear weak. Instead, say, "Fine," and prepare so well for a court hearing that you will settle only if it's truly beneficial to you. Blamers and negative-advocate attorneys need to know that you and your attorney are willing to set firm limits when necessary.

# Settlement Conferences

Many family court systems offer or require settlement conferences prior to trials on the issues in a divorce. This is generally a confidential process, and the settlement judge (or experienced settlement attorney) should be different from the trial judge. The settlement judge informally meets with the parties and their attorneys at court on a separate date before the trial. The settlement judge makes recommendations to the parties about how the case should be settled, based on the law and her view of a realistic agreement.

The parties don't have to agree, and the option remains open to go to trial on some or all issues, starting fresh with the trial judge who has not heard your negotiations. This tends to work well for mild and moderate blamers, because there is a lot of realistic information and it's easier for partners with BP, NP, or ASP traits to accept a recommended settlement from a neutral authority figure, rather than a proposal from the hated other party or that person's attorney. But severe blamers often still want to fight and won't settle many or any issues, even if a settlement judge encourages them to do so. They believe that their way of thinking is the only right way, and they cannot accept any other resolution.

## Arbitration or Private Trial

Arbitration is different from mediation, although the terms are often confused and interchanged. In arbitration, the arbitrator makes the decisions (like a judge), while in mediation the parties make the decisions, and the mediator simply helps them. Arbitration is allowed in some jurisdictions for some divorce issues, primarily regarding property division.

Arbitration is an abbreviated form of a trial, in which both parties present their cases. Then the arbitrator decides the case based on legal precedent and law. Though quicker and less expensive than court, arbitration is often subject to court approval, because only a judge may make the final decisions on matters such as child custody and visitation. The benefit of arbitration is that many blamers will accept a neutral authority's decision or recommendation, whereas they are not comfortable proposing concessions or making agreements themselves; it makes them feel too powerless, abandoned, or out of control.

A private trial usually involves a retired judge. The parties can keep their case out of the public eye for one reason or another. It saves money, and it can occur much more quickly than an ordinary trial. If the parties have the funds, they can arrange to hire a mutually agreeable decision maker and spend a day or two having their decisions made with more of the parties' participation than may occur in a regular trial.

The rules can be more flexible, and the judge can get to know the parties better. The benefit of this approach is that it saves money and time and is more private than the "day in court" the blamer often seeks. Drawbacks may include limits on the types of issues that can be resolved in this manner. Further, a complete decision by a hired judge may satisfy one party and not the other. Then you have the issue of appeals, set-asides, or motions at regular courts to modify the decision the hired judge made. So this approach may or may not work with an angry blamer.

## New Ways for Families

New Ways for Families® is a new program Bill developed for any family going through a potentially high-conflict divorce involving children. It was specifically designed for families in which a parent may have a PD, but it can be helpful to any family. It is a short-term counseling method, before the big, long-term decisions are made by a judge or out of court. The focus is on skills before decisions. Each parent has an individual parent counselor who uses a workbook to focus the parent on practicing three big skills for conflict resolution: flexible thinking, managed emotions, and moderate behaviors. Then, each parent meets with the children and teaches them the same skills.

By involving both parents in this process before big decisions are made, there is the chance that a blamer will be less defensive and more open to practicing these positive skills. A reasonable parent also benefits from this short-term counseling, because it teaches skills for dealing with a difficult parent (including one with BPD, NPD, or ASPD).

A few years after establishing the counseling method, it became clear that an online course for teaching these skills would reach many more people and would reduce the cost. Information about all of the New Ways for Families® models can be found in the Resources section at the end of this book.

## Parenting Coordinator

Parenting coordination is a method increasingly used for managing parenting conflict out of court, *after* the big decisions and custody arrangements have been made. The parenting coordinator (PC) helps the parents interpret the court-ordered parenting plan and communicate regarding switching access or visitation days and making changes in the future. The parenting coordinator resolves any disputes in these matters. Many reasonable parents have found this to be an effective way to manage a blamer, who may want to keep the conflict going even after all the big decisions have been made. It's also possible to combine learning and practicing the skills from New Ways for Families® with parenting coordination, so that the PC can remind the blamer (and you) to use reasonable conflict-resolution skills each time a new problem arises.

## Priorities to Consider

First, with mild and moderate blamers, try a mediator. If a skilled mediator cannot make progress, try a collaborative divorce for mild, moderate, and severe blamers. If skilled collaborative professionals cannot succeed at reaching a settlement, then use

separate negotiating attorneys, a private retired judge, or both
to make recommendations or binding decisions out of court.

When considering these alternatives, consult with an attorney, a therapist, or both to assess which approach may be most
successful with your blamer partner. Try at least one out-of-
court alternative before risking the negativity and escalation
of conflict that results from going to court. Perhaps you can
persuade your blamer to agree, if for no other reason than to
try to save money and avoid public humiliation. You will have
more control over the process, the pace, and the decisions of
your case out of court. This is not always possible with blamers,
especially severe ones. Don't feel as though you have to settle
your case if the blamer is making extreme demands.

*When Thomas told Tammy he wanted to get a divorce,
he suggested that they use mediation to save money and
work together. In response, she threw an iron at him and
smashed a window in his car. He and his attorney believed
that Tammy might have severe BPD, so instead they filed
for a hearing at court to resolve the issues.*

*Thomas's attorney knew that Tammy's attorney had a
reputation for escalating conflict in divorce cases. But they
were still required to talk at court before the first hearing.
Since Tammy and her attorney supported the Family Court
Services counselor's recommendation for supervised visitation
for Thomas, the best Thomas's attorney could negotiate at
that point was who the supervisor would be. It was their only
agreement, and Thomas's attorney told him to prepare for a
lot of court battles ahead.*

*Sarah hired an attorney after the judge gave Sam custody
and her restraining order was thrown out. Her attorney was
familiar with Sam's attorney, and they decided it would be
best for her attorney to initiate a telephone dialogue. It went*

like this: "Hi, Bob; this is Brett. I'm going to represent Sarah now. I am very concerned about her and am thinking about bringing another request for a restraining order against Sam. There's a lot of history that hasn't come out yet that will be damaging to your client. I'd rather not escalate the case. Are you open to discussion?"

"Sure, Brett. I know there are always two sides to every story. Tell me what you think is going on, and I'll discuss it with Sam. I'd rather just do it over the phone, so we don't have all those nasty letters going back and forth, pushing our clients' buttons. He's a pretty sensitive guy."

Both Bob and Brett had experience at trying to reduce tensions and negotiating agreements in family law cases. In this case, there were abuse issues, and their clients were the main decision makers, so they ended up starting out in court, and then forming an out-of-court settlement.

# Blamers and Compromise

Blamers are not usually good at negotiation and other forms of compromise. They engage in all-or-nothing thinking, personalize even the most minor issues, and may feel that "giving in" to the other party's requests is a form of abandonment or threat to their superiority. For these reasons, alternatives to court may not be successful. The blamer may feel that he is participating in accepting a loss he cannot tolerate. People with borderline traits think they must refuse compromise to avoid feeling abandoned, whereas people with narcissistic traits see themselves as superior and feel they should receive more.

Blamers may be the only people in today's world who "want to" go to court, because they believe they can be persuasive. They may be willing to take their chances, even when advised against it by their support people and professionals. So you may end up in court, unless you give in to the blamer's unreasonable demands. Since this is such a strong temptation for people who are used to "walking on eggshells," the next section is devoted to this issue.

## Deciding Whether to Settle or Fight

Many targets of blame are so used to giving in to avoid an argument or abuse that standing firm or fighting is a new concept. Yet in a court case, the stakes are so much higher that you should make this decision only with the advice of your attorney, therapist, and support people. Otherwise, you can permanently give up legal rights or get stuck with a history of "true findings" that you're an abusive person or someone who makes false allegations, even if you're not. Your future depends on consistently asserting the truth and your rights.

> *Sarah told her attorney, Brett, that she didn't care about the house or monthly spousal support. All she cared about was having custody of her son, Jay. She feared for Jay, because Sam usually lost interest in him except when there was a fight. "Can't we just tell him I'll give up everything else if he gives me custody and a little child support? I can get a job. My cousin will help. I'll just agree that the house is his," she said.*
>
> *Brett replied, "I don't advise that, because you have a lot of rights. You have some financial interest in the house, possibly an equal interest. Just because the deed is in his name does not resolve the issue. He may have manipulated you to sign the deed, and it may not be valid. He may have paid for the mortgage with income during the marriage.*
>
> *"If what you tell me is true about his abuse of you and your generally good care of Jay, then you should have custody.*

*You may be used to giving up a lot for the sake of peace with Sam, but now is not the time to do that. You can always decide later to give up something small for the sake of a final settlement, but at the beginning you should be as strong as possible."*

*Sarah seemed worried. "Well, I don't want to bring up his drinking problem and talk about the bruises. That would really upset him. And I don't want to ask for another restraining order."*

*Brett pointed out that Sam had gotten custody because these issues had not been brought out. He told Sarah, "For the sake of your child, you need to let these decisions be based on the full facts, rather than the impression the court now has that you're the target of blame for everything."*

*A year before Thomas told Tammy he wanted a divorce, they had a big argument. Tammy was so angry that she just started punching him in the chest. He grabbed her wrists and pushed her down on the bed to restrain her. After she calmed down, he went into the bathroom to be away from her for a few minutes.*

*While Thomas was in the bathroom, Tammy called the police without his knowledge. The police came, and she reported a dramatic assault and battery. A temporary restraining order was issued against Thomas with a court hearing in five days. He stayed at his mother's house until the hearing.*

*To keep the peace, Thomas considered simply accepting the restraining order, because he did not want to spend the time or money it would take to fight it. He knew Tammy was capable of saying anything in court, and he did not want either of them to be embarrassed. He was considering divorce anyhow, so this could be the time to do it.*

*But then he spoke with an attorney, who advised him that it would permanently hurt him to admit to something he had not done. So Thomas went to court with his attorney and submitted a detailed declaration of what had occurred, in response to Tammy's rambling and blaming declaration. The judge found his information to be more credible, and Tammy started yelling at the judge, which reinforced that she was the aggressive party.*

*After the restraining order was dropped, Tammy pleaded with Thomas to come back home—and he did, for a year. When the divorce began and Tammy made her sexual abuse allegations, Thomas was extremely glad he had been talked out of stipulating to the restraining order. He had enough to deal with without a false legal history.*

Each issue in a divorce case can be settled or decided in court. Family courts allow you to give in and make bad agreements, since you're adults with the opportunity to get legal advice. Family courts are not criminal courts, so the judge rarely looks into whether or not your settlement is one-sided, unfair, or unjust.

There are several factors to consider regarding fighting in court against someone with BP, NP, or ASP traits.

## The Risks of Giving In

One of the most common questions we receive in emails from around the country is whether to stipulate (sign a formal agreement) to restraining orders based on false allegations. In the past, stipulating to restraining orders based on a false allegation of domestic violence carried few consequences. So, many attorneys advised their clients to do so, especially when an unpredictable partner with BP, NP, or ASP traits was involved, rather than go through the time, money, and embarrassment of a public court hearing. The target just agreed to stay at least one hundred yards away, because that person wanted to stay away anyway.

Nowadays, there can be many long-term negative consequences affecting child-custody rights, monthly support obligations, and employment. In family court matters, many issues are discretionary with the judge. Having a "history" of violence, child abuse, and so forth can be used against you for years (or decades), even though they are based on totally false allegations. In addition, having a history of making false allegations can ruin your credibility on all other issues. It's very hard to undo such damage later on with the same judge, or even a new judge.

## What Are Your Long-Term Goals?

Long-term peace is not won by making large concessions to people with BP, NP, or ASP traits, because of their cognitive distortions. They expect to receive huge concessions because everything is "all your fault" in their eyes. When you give in, they just want more. In fact, when targets stop making concessions is when blamers often initiate litigation. It's best to prepare for court from the start, rather than make large, unnecessary concessions to avoid court.

Determine whether your expectations are realistic. It's helpful to consult with an attorney who will be very realistic with you. In many cases, it's helpful to get a second opinion from another attorney. The law has very specific rules about legal issues and legal outcomes. You will need to find out whether your expectations are even legally possible.

A lifetime restraining order against a blamer is very unlikely. In some states, a "permanent" restraining order means three years or less. If you expect the court to change the person's daily behavior, you should know by now that this is not likely with a blamer. A court can order a sanction or fine for misconduct, but it is incapable of changing the conduct itself. As we know about people with PDs, one consequence does not change a lifetime pattern of harmful behavior.

## Court Will Push the Blamer's Buttons

Blamers feel especially threatened in adversarial situations where there may be consequences for their behavior. Unlike the home or work environment, where they may be tolerated and their misconduct may be ignored or placated, at court the threat of consequences is very real and therefore frightening to the blamer (and everyone else). The feeling most often triggered is that of abandonment or inferiority.

## Get Ready for Escalating Allegations

Ironically, the more successful you are in court at presenting the facts, the more extreme the blamer's counterattack will be in terms of abusive behavior or allegations against you. Because the court must seriously consider each allegation, you will frequently feel that the process is one step forward, one step back. Depending on the blamer, this experience may be more like one step forward, three steps back. In deciding whether to take the blamer to court, you must consider how persuasive his allegations are. You probably already have some experience in this area.

## Documentation and Credible Witnesses

The way to survive and win in court is with verifiable, clearcut facts. This is usually in the form of documents, credible witnesses, and knowledgeable experts or evaluators. You should have at least one credible professional on your side before beginning a court case against a blamer, in addition to your attorney. This could be a therapist, a teacher, an accountant, or another professional. You must decide whether such documents and witnesses are available to you.

Some professionals start out biased or become emotionally "hooked" during court cases and take an extreme position for or against one or the other party. They present themselves not as objective, but rather passionately promoting a political agenda. They lose credibility by appearing to be swayed by impressions rather than facts. You are most benefited by a professional who has a reputation with the court for objectivity and is able to calmly provide narrow, specific information that is very relevant to your case.

## Can You Cope with Hearing Perjury?

Many of the interpersonal issues about which blamers make allegations are very hard to challenge with facts. Therefore, you must determine whether it's worthwhile to engage in a "he said, she said" type of case at court. At times, these cases make your life much more difficult and provide a very unsatisfying outcome. Family courts rarely make findings that a party has committed perjury or is lying. Instead, they simply weigh the credibility of each side and make decisions about what to do in the future or what consequences to impose from the past. So don't be surprised if the court occasionally makes excuses for the other party or minimizes the significance of that person's doubtful statements.

## Consider Financial Concessions

In some cases, targets have said later on that they would have given in to a blamer's early financial demands if they had realized how much time and money court can cost. We don't necessarily recommend this, but small concessions are something to consider in each case—except when the physical and mental health of a child is at stake. A key factor to consider is whether the disputed issue is a narrow and small one that may be resolved by one financial settlement. If there are no children and you expect to sever all ties, it may be wise to make a settlement for an amount you can live with and get the battle over quickly. You may save money in the long run.

## Are You Willing to Set Limits?

If you will have an ongoing relationship with the blamer, such as sharing custody or visitation of your children, you may want to fight hard so that your partner's behavior begins to know limits and consequences. In some cases, you may wish to fight the blamer in court even if you're likely to lose on a particular issue. The purpose of fighting may be to show the blamer that there's no benefit to future threats of going to court. You will teach the blamer that you're willing to match her aggressiveness with assertiveness, if necessary. You can also show that you will disclose the blamer's abusive private behavior, if any. This exposure may be the best deterrent against future problems.

## Do You Have the Stamina?

Remember, energy is an important part of our recommendations: the first "E" in KEEP CALM. Many people get worn down by the blamer even before going to court. At court, there will probably be one or more negative advocates working for the blamer, evaluators who may like the blamer better than you in the short run, and judges who will never know very much about the realities of your case. If you're aware of this and prepared for it, then you have a much better chance of winning in the short run and preventing future similar behavior from the blamer.

## Are You Willing to Tell All?

Most targets who have been involved with a blamer for a long period of time have tolerated a great deal of misbehavior, abuse, and possibly violence from the blamer. Yet it's common for targets to want to hold back from exposing all of this misbehavior. You may be worried that confronting the blamer will escalate the blaming, while holding back negative feedback has calmed her down in the past. (You also may have engaged in behavior you're not proud of and don't want to expose.)

If the blamer has already engaged you in a battle, you will need to present all of the necessary information that will help the court understand what's going on: fully explaining patterns of unchanging harmful behavior. Be prepared for the possibility that your attorney, court experts, and the judge will disregard the information—initially. You must be willing to back up your information with credible evidence, such as a witness or verifying documents. Remember, family court is an adversarial setting, and you will need to be very assertive to succeed. The judge cannot know what you don't tell her. But once it becomes clear that you are willing to be highly assertive in court, the blamer may become more willing to settle out of court.

## Conclusion

Confronting a blamer in court can take a few months or many years. It can cost a lot, in terms of time, money, and emotional distress. Therefore, in most cases, it's worth it to try to manage the blamer with an out-of-court alternative, like mediation, collaborative divorce, negotiations with attorneys, New Ways for Families®, or a parenting coordinator.

With a severe blamer (lots of false allegations or abusive behavior), it often costs less if you fight assertively at the start and are prepared for anything. Unless you can get a reasonable out-of-court settlement in a reasonable period of time, fighting in court may be your best option. At all times, when dealing with a partner with possible BPD, NPD, or ASPD, choose your battles wisely and get lots of consultation from professionals and support from your support people—every step of the way.

*Chapter 16*

# Managing the Rocky Postdivorce Relationship

With many blamers, the cycle of your postdivorce relationship may look a lot like your marriage and a lot like your divorce: a roller coaster of good times, intense confrontation, explosions, and momentary peace. If there are no children involved, there may be a slow growing apart, as the blamer gets involved with other people and other dramas. But until the blamer becomes involved in a new intense relationship, you will probably remain a target of attention, controversy, and blame. Part of this will focus on the blamer's disregard for the positive court orders you've obtained, your need to attempt to modify negative court orders, and your personal interactions over time. Managing this relationship is the "M" in KEEP CALM.

## Enforcing Court Orders with a Blamer

Suppose you succeeded in family court and the judge truly understood the underlying dynamics of your case and made very appropriate court orders. Yet with a blamer who isn't in treatment, enforcing your court orders may be extremely difficult. People with BP traits often feel abandoned by the court's decisions, and those with NP tendencies see themselves as superior to any court's orders. Their behavior often suggests that they consider themselves a law unto themselves. Enforcement methods are highly specific to your state laws. The following are some general measures to consider.

## Kidnapping by a Parent

Most of the parental kidnapping cases Bill has experienced or observed seem to involve people with narcissistic or antisocial personalities, or both, who decided they were above the law and felt they had the right to take matters into their own hands to prevent behavior they believed was abusive on the other party's part—even when the court disagreed. States and countries have agreed on parental kidnapping laws to prevent "splitting" between court jurisdictions caused by probable blamers.

Therefore, enforcement of custody and visitation orders has grown much stronger over the past few years at all levels. Most states have adopted the Uniform Child Custody Jurisdiction and Enforcement Act (UCCJEA), which requires state courts to respect and enforce the custody and visitation orders of other states. These laws also restrict the ability of a new state's courts to modify the orders made in the first state.

In addition, there are criminal penalties if a parent takes a child out of state in violation of the other parent's custody or visitation rights. These laws are growing stronger every year. Many of the cases that led to the creation of these laws involved parents with symptoms of a PD:

- An unwillingness to share parenting

- An enmeshed relationship with a child

- A sense of superiority to the court's orders

- Impulsive, self-destructive behaviors

Internationally, over fifty countries have signed on to the Hague Convention on the Civil Aspects of International Child Abduction. The rules of this convention are designed to protect children from wrongful removal to or retention in a different country by a parent. You have probably heard about some high-profile cases in the news that involved these rules and laws. Of course, there are exceptions for emergencies and real endangerment, but the courts are getting wiser about alleged emergencies because blamers often allege "emergencies."

## Visitation or Access Orders

Many parents are frustrated when a blamer completely ignores court orders regarding children. Says one target, "He routinely comes late to pick up the children and return them. He tells them it doesn't matter what the court orders say" (possible narcissist feeling superior). Another complained, "She's rarely home when I come to pick up the children, or I have to wait around when I bring them back. She says if I hadn't divorced her, we wouldn't have these problems" (possibly has BP traits and feels abandoned).

The consequences for these types of manipulative violations of court orders are limited. No court is likely to put a parent in jail for this, and parents are rarely fined for such "minor" infractions. But it isn't uncommon for blamers to engage in numerous "minor" infractions, as they manipulatively resist an order they know they should give the appearance of following.

The usual enforcement methods for visitation exchanges are to return to court for new visitation orders. The court may decide to reduce the visitation or require the use of a visitation exchange supervisor. Supervisors receive the child from one parent, who then leaves, and then the other parent arrives to pick up the child. This neutral third party reduces the allegations and increases the consistency of the schedule. Of course, this costs the parties money, but it may save court costs in the long run.

Often the best thing to do is keep a journal of problems that arise, including dates and times. Note any witnesses present and what the other party may have said. The next time there is a court hearing to modify custody or visitation, you can include this information in your declaration. If you focus on facts rather than drama or labels, the court may see you as the more reasonable party. But the other party may be keeping the same kind of records. The best solution is to make sure you carefully follow the court orders and contact your attorney if there's a reason why you can't.

## Support Orders

Child support is now one of the most enforceable court orders in the country. Federal laws make sure child support is paid, requiring standardized forms, mutual enforcement between the states, and reporting to the federal government. Some states have automatic child-support orders that require support to be deducted from the payer's wages. This order can be sent to the payer's employer, so that the employer deducts the funds and sends them to the receiving parent.

Sometimes cooperative parties may agree that this wage deduction isn't necessary. The payments may be sent directly by check or even automatic bank withdrawal. But if this process fails, the wage deduction order is already available to be sent to the employer.

Spousal support (alimony) is also enforceable by a wage garnishment order, but the federal government hasn't become involved in this.

Support payments remain an obligation until they are paid. So enforcement actions may be begun at any time, even years later. In addition, many states require a person in arrears to pay additional interest, penalties, and attorney fees for the party bringing the matter back to court.

## No Mutual Violations Allowed

Since blamers routinely violate custody, visitation, support orders, or all of these, targets are often tempted to violate other orders to balance things out: "If he won't pay me the proper support, then I shouldn't let him see the children," or, "If she won't follow the visitation orders, then I'll withhold the support payments until she does."

The courts specifically prohibit this tit-for-tat approach (where would it end?), so even if one parent is "frustrating" visitation, the other parent must pay full support. There may be exceptions for "concealment" of a child through illegal abduction or violation of rules regarding international moves. Check with your attorney. Likewise, a parent can't withhold the children from the court-ordered visitation, even if child support hasn't been paid. The remedy in these cases is to return to court for new orders in each area.

## Retirement Plans

One of the biggest assets a couple may have acquired during the marriage is a retirement plan in one partner's name. Both partners may have shared rights in such a plan, which are usually spelled out in the final divorce orders. A qualified domestic relations order (QDRO) is commonly prepared, dividing the account into each party's respective share according to federal regulations.

There's always the risk that the partner whose name is on the plan will be tempted to withdraw the funds before the court can make such an order. So an attorney may implement a joinder of the retirement plan to the divorce case as soon as the divorce case is filed. A notice is sent to the employer or administrator of the plan to freeze the plan until further court orders may be made. This has become routine in many cases; it doesn't imply mistrust. It's simply a step to go through in completing the divorce. Regardless, it protects the other party if there are any concerns.

## Attaching Accounts or Other Assets

Once the court has made an order that one party owes the other party money or an asset, there are measures for obtaining these funds or assets against that person's will. This may involve having a marshal serve a writ of execution or similar order on a bank or other institution. Proper procedures must be followed to accomplish this.

## Liens on Real Estate

When seeking financial orders, you will need a mechanism to secure that you're paid if there are property payments over time. One of the easiest and most common methods is to put a lien on any real estate that the other party may acquire in the divorce. Suppose your partner will receive the house in the divorce but owes you fifty thousand dollars as an equalizing payment, which will be paid over time (often with interest). You sign over the deed, giving your partner sole ownership of the house. Your partner signs a promissory note and deed of trust, securing your right to be paid fifty thousand dollars. Then you exchange these documents. You can record your deed of trust with the county where the property is located, and the house can't be sold until you receive your payment. This is always a good idea, even if you trust each other, because the person's future spouses or heirs may try to ignore such a payment to you if it isn't required.

## Contempt of Court Orders

Many people are familiar with the concept of contempt of court. This is a broad term for many types of enforcement orders. Most commonly it is a method to maintain control in the courtroom. The judge might say, "If you don't stop speaking right now, I will hold you in contempt of the court, and you will spend the night in jail." The violation of any court order may be treated as though you are in contempt of court orders.

Contempt procedures are quasi-criminal in nature rather than civil, so most judges don't like to use them because they're so burdensome. Many more rules must be followed than for most other family court procedures. The burden of proof may be higher, and the accused may be able to plead the Fifth Amendment rather than testify against himself, but it is an enforcement measure and may be appropriate or necessary.

Nonpayment of child and spousal support may be enforced by contempt against a self-employed or unemployed person. The specific consequences and benefits of contempt are limited. There may be up to five days in jail or a fine of one thousand dollars for each offense, depending on state laws. If a person is found to be in contempt for two years of monthly support payments, that could add up to twenty-four thousand dollars.

If the person evaded paying the underlying support order, she is likely to evade the contempt order as well. It's also unlikely that the court will put the person in jail, because it would prevent her from working and paying off the debt, but jail has a motivating effect on most people, and a realistic threat of jail time, no matter how brief, may inspire sudden payment. This enforcement measure is most effective against big-time violators, such as the wealthy person with narcissistic traits who owes more than one hundred thousand dollars in back support payments and has the obvious assets to pay it, but just doesn't want to follow the court's order because of a feeling of special-ness and superiority.

Contempt is seen as inappropriate for use in custody and visitation matters. The courts don't want to interfere with parental contact and don't want it to become a daily weapon in these disputes. In Bill's experience, judges who make a rare finding of contempt in such cases give a suspended sentence.

## Sanctions

Sanctions may be a better alternative to contempt in most cases. This involves having one party pay the other party's attorney fees as a punishment for unnecessary litigation or other improper court-case-related misconduct. This is a civil measure within the court's discretion, so it is less complicated and can be made to fit the specific misconduct. Parties may be sanctioned one hundred dollars or one hundred thousand dollars, depending on their ability and the behavior. Judges use sanctions cautiously, although their use seems to be increasing.

In many cases, just the credible threat of sanctions may slow down a misbehaving blamer. Blamers don't like to look bad and don't like to give the opposing party money. Describing the misconduct in a letter or declaration, followed by a quote from the local sanctions law, has had a positive impact on some blamers. Blamers may then counter with some claim of misconduct against you, escalating the request for sanctions. Don't use this approach lightly, or your credibility with the other party and the court may be weakened.

## Summary of Enforcement Methods

Research all of the previous enforcement measures and use them when appropriate. Frequent, empty threats to enforce court orders may do you more harm than good, but careful threats can get the blamer's attention, because blamers want to maintain their public persona.

Plan ahead and be ready to implement enforcement actions before the blamer can disappear with the children, quit his job, or dispose of assets. Discuss enforcement issues with your attorney before you start your case or as soon as possible.

## Modifying Prior Court Orders

After a bad court decision, you may be tempted to find a way to undo it. As they say on television, "We're going to fight this all the way to the Supreme Court." But these are often empty threats, made to save face or vent frustration. Undoing a court order can be very difficult, which is why you should put all your efforts into getting the best court orders from the start.

Modifications are simple and appropriate as a child grows up, incomes change, or both. If you can be patient, you may be able to get a better decision after you have let some time pass or gathered better evidence, or after some circumstances have changed.

At a hearing, the court ordered a fifty-fifty parenting schedule for a couple's eight-year-old daughter, over the mother's objections. The mother had concerns because the father was very self-absorbed, narcissistic, and preoccupied with work. He talked the talk about being an "equal" parent, but wouldn't walk the walk. The mother had argued that the child preferred to live with her. The blamer argued that the mother was alienating the child against him. The court counselor met with the child, who said she loved both parents and didn't care how much time she spent with each (a diplomatic child, as many feel they have to be in these cases).

The court counselor recommended equal custody, noting the father's concerns that the mother was alienating the child from him. At a subsequent hearing, the mother requested that the child have a therapist. In therapy, the girl described various problems in the father's home. It appeared that he had lost interest in the child after court and that he spent most of his time at work. The therapist spoke with the father, who admitted these problems but belittled the child's concerns and blamed the mother.

It became clear to the therapist that the mother's concerns were reasonable and that she was not attempting to alienate the child from the father. The father's own admitted behavior was the problem, and he was unwilling to change.

A year after the initial fifty-fifty parenting order, the mother brought the matter back to court for a modification. Both parents authorized the court counselor to speak with the child's therapist. The court counselor agreed with the child's therapist and recommended more time with the mother based on this change of circumstances. The judge agreed and gave the mother primary physical custody.

## Motions to Reconsider or Set Aside

In extreme circumstances, the court may reconsider a decision or set it aside. The procedures for this action are governed by state laws and are very narrow and specific because of the emphasis on stability of court orders so that people aren't back in court every month challenging the prior month's orders. Such motions should be used only on the clear advice of an attorney and if there's a chance of success. They are based on legal technicalities, not on the argument that the judge merely made a bad decision.

## Appeals

A formal appeal goes to the court of appeals overseeing cases in your geographical region. In almost all family court cases, these are state courts of appeal. The state supreme court is the final decision maker regarding most family law matters, but few cases get to that level. Instead, there is a district court of appeals that's most likely to be the end of the case. A family court appeal may succeed in only about 20 percent of cases, at best, according to reports in one district at a seminar Bill attended, presented by members of the local court of appeals. An appeal of a family law matter may require a technical error or an extreme "abuse of discretion" by the judge. In other words, a bad decision isn't a basis for an appeal. The appeals courts are not supposed to take a fresh look at the factual content of the decision; rather, they look to see whether the judge followed the rules in the process of making the decision.

In an international move-away case, the judge made a decision that gave jurisdiction to the new country's court. But the law under which the decision was made had recently changed, and the judge did not follow all the steps of the procedure. The court of appeals reversed the move-away decision based solely on the trial court's omission of some steps required by the new law.

While you may have a chance of success in an appeal, it can cost a lot of money and time. Appeals can take one to five years, and the research and argument involved can cost as much or more than the underlying hearing or trial.

## Acceptance

Sometimes the best approach is to work on acceptance of the court's orders by talking about your frustrations during sessions with your therapist. You may be absolutely correct that the orders were bad and that the court completely misunderstood the dynamics of your case and the personalities involved. But sometimes nothing more can be done. Have a heart-to-heart talk with your attorney about whether it might be better to move on and let go of a losing battle.

This may be a time to focus on doing the best you can with your situation. Make the most of your time with your child. Your positive influence may outweigh the harm you fear the other parent will do. Your finances may be terribly squeezed for quite a while, but people learn to live on less. Many people report that their finances are better a couple of years after the divorce. Someone who is able to accept matters and move on is often better able to provide nurturing and a positive role model to her children than a person who remains stuck in a hopeless battle, frustrated by impossible expectations.

Even when there have been bad court decisions creating a significant limitation on child contact, the destruction of finances, or both, we have seen many targets develop a healthy attitude and rebound in their lives. It is often blamers who have the hardest time with acceptance—even when they have "won." Their cognitive distortions prevent them from processing new information and relaxing, so that they're stuck fighting old battles with whoever will listen.

People who allow themselves to feel like helpless victims of the court lead sadder lives than those who look at what they can do with the cards they are dealt. As some have learned to say, "It's a therapy issue now, isn't it?"


# Your Postdivorce Relationship

Just because you're divorced doesn't mean the borderline, narcissistic, or antisocial partner has let you go. Be very careful in all future dealings. Be moderate: not too friendly, not too abrupt. Here are some things to keep in mind while you manage this relationship.

## Avoid Being Too Close

It's common for targets to feel relieved by the end of the divorce process, then to relax and attempt to develop a somewhat close friendship with the "ex." Sometimes they even have sex. Resist this urge. This can be misleading to a person with BP traits, who assumes you want to get back together and then attacks you for disappointing her. A person with narcissistic traits may take advantage of you and try to get you to do favors.

## Avoid Being Too Rejecting

Some targets are so glad to be free of the years of intensity and blame that they almost refuse to talk to their blamers. If there are no children and no other issues tying you together, this may be your goal. But you may want to ease the transition a little by at least being civil. Abruptness can trigger the abandonment issues and related defense mechanisms of a person with BP traits and can be a narcissistic injury to someone with narcissistic traits, as explained in chapter 2.

## Arm's-Length Relationship

An "arm's-length" relationship works best: consistent and civil, no confusing intimacy or hostile distance. You can be nice, but don't imply the type of "relationship" that rekindles confusing emotions. If you're co-parenting, you will have many contacts over the children. You can be friendly and sympathetic if your former partner shares good or bad news with you, but don't get overly involved and open up, and don't appear too insensitive and hostile. While you have no obligation, it may make your life easier to maintain an arm's-length interest in whatever is shared with you. Many blamers report feeling offended by the ex's seeming disinterest in their ups and downs, and they unconsciously find a way to retaliate.

## New Battles

Most high-conflict divorce cases can remain high conflict for years after the divorce. Remember, blamers have great difficulty with healing from loss and letting go. When your ex is just as angry or sad about the divorce more than two years after it's over, it is almost a certain indicator of a PD.

Positive new events (remarriage, new baby, career success) in your life may trigger a blamer to feel great sadness, loss, fear, intense anger, or all of these emotions. Blamers may feel that they have to punish you or exert some kind of control over you to keep you engaged in their lives. In fact, many of the most extreme false allegations seem to come after the divorce.

Keep good records of parenting problems, confrontations, and visitation-exchange behavior. If inappropriate behavior starts building, let the blamer know that you won't hesitate to call your attorney or return to court if necessary. But try to balance this firmness with a friendly word or two to avoid escalating the person's emotions too much.

## Future Custody Disputes

One of the main disputes in postdivorce litigation is child custody. Even if you handled custody and visitation by out-of-court agreement in your divorce, the dynamics can change as you get on with your new life. After the divorce, some people with BP traits seem to shift their dependency needs onto the child. Yet at the same time, the child is growing up and exerting greater independence. This can feel "abandoning" to the person with BP traits, whether the child is three or eight years old. Since that person is dependent on the child, she can't allow herself to blame the child for these natural moves toward independence. Therefore, it must be "all your fault."

The person's cognitive distortions get triggered, and all kinds of extreme thoughts may get generated, including allegations of abuse by you. People with BP tendencies seem to desire the elimination of the other parent as much as possible, stating that you're a "threat" to the child for some reason, and you need supervised visitation or no contact. Since these types of orders are used only when there are serious abuse allegations, people with BP, NP, or ASP traits often make very serious abuse allegations. This entire process may be totally unconscious, although some blamers are willing to make knowingly false statements to accomplish their desperate goals.

It seems that many narcissists also project their internal issues onto the children. There's very little else that they have control over in their lives, and they are constantly having relationship failures because of their self-centeredness. Thus, they see increased time with their children as a solution. Also, being a custodial parent boosts a person's image and self-image in today's world.

Many people with narcissistic tendencies are preoccupied with new relationships at the time of the divorce, so they are fairly flexible in allowing custody with the other parent. Then, after some setbacks in their new relationships or business dealings, they often act to get custody postdivorce. This process may be totally unconscious, although they also may be willing to make some knowingly false statements to accomplish their goals.

The previous analyses are possible explanations of why intense custody battles seem to arise two years, even five years, after the divorce. These years may have been ones of relative peace. What has changed isn't the relationship between the ex-partners but, rather, the blamer's other adult relationships, possibly including relationship failures or the creation of a new family. In either case, blamers seek increased power and control over the children, the only "constant object" in their lives.

None of this section's commentary is intended to discount parents' protective actions in response to real external events, such as moves, abuse by new relationship partners, or other external risks to a child. Our message is that much of post-divorce litigation is driven by the blamer's predictable internal life developments, not external events.

## Future Custody Battles

Some of the worst child-custody battles occur after the divorce is over. The following is an example of some dynamics Bill has seen in numerous cases. In many of these cases, the blamer has appeared to have some of the antisocial personality traits described in chapter 2, as well as BP, NP, or ASP traits. Remember, people with antisocial personalities lack empathy (even more than those with narcissistic personalities) and see situations in terms of short-term personal gain, regardless of its effect on others. They enjoy dominating others and fear being dominated. This sequence may help explain this pattern so you can avoid it.

1. There is a history of several years of fairly noncontro-versial primary parenting by the target. There may never have been a custody dispute before, and the divorce may even have been handled through an out-of-court marital settlement agreement. The blamer has had no serious complaints about the target's parenting.

2. The blamer's emotional involvement with the child or children has been minimal or negative, even though there may be regular contact.

3.  The blamer is usually self-employed or unemployed, or works primarily alone, with the ability to control most aspects of her life and finances.

4.  A financial pressure occurs for the blamer, in the form of a request for support or an increase in support made by the target. Or it may be triggered by a business loss or financial problems in a new relationship. The blamer feels threatened.

5.  The blamer secretly takes the children into confidence. He promises trips, sporting events, cool gear, and so on. He also reinforces or encourages criticisms of the target: "She can really be bossy and irritating, can't she?" "He can really be annoying and controlling, can't he?" These criticisms often focus on bonding with the child in an adolescent manner around issues of independence against the target's "authority."

6.  The blamer and child form a fun, childlike conspiracy against the target, keeping secrets and doing "forbidden" but fun deeds. The child feels torn, but it's often easier to side with a demanding parent against a fairly accepting and unsuspecting target. The child has more to risk in challenging the blamer (whom the child wishes to have a closer relationship with) than the target (whom the child usually has a comfortable relationship with). The sense of grown-up freedom the blamer provides is also enticing.

7.  The child writes a letter to the judge or declaration to the court against the target with vague or unfounded complaints. Or the child makes vague complaints to a therapist or Family Court Services counselor against the target. The child often uses the antisocial blamer's

words ("too annoying" or "too controlling"). The blamer pressures the court to let the child testify against the target. (This alone is one of the most insensitive acts a parent can do, indicating a strong lack of empathy.)

8. The blamer takes a therapist into her confidence, who will see the child without requiring the target's consent. The blamer may report a crisis requiring secrecy from the other parent "to protect the child." The blamer will ask the therapist to write a letter to the court because of the "crisis." The therapist may recommend counseling, but the blamer doesn't follow through. That's not his goal.

9. The blamer may involve other children or adults in building a case against the target. The blamer tells them that extreme events will occur without their help. (In one case, an apparently antisocial parent got a whole children's soccer team to write letters to the judge, requesting to overturn a prior court order.)

10. The blamer manipulates court procedures, by not notifying the other parent of court hearings, trying to get emergency hearings, trying to change evaluators or judges, or going to different courts in other jurisdictions on the same issues.

The apparent catalyst in many of these cases is the target's request to reduce (if paying) or obtain child support. But the underlying emotional drive appears to be the antisocial person's fear of being dominated by the target or desire to dominate the target. People with antisocial traits apply their antisocial skills to "con" the court, and they are often successful. They are con artists.

In some of these cases, the blamer persuades the courts that the target's parenting is harmful or that a rift has occurred in the target's relationship with the children, even though that is completely untrue. Custody is changed to the parent with antisocial tendencies. In other cases, the target is able to block or limit the change of custody.

Within a year of such a custody change, there are reports that the children are depressed. They appear to feel trapped in the manipulative power of the parent with antisocial traits, yet unwilling to confront that parent because of their worn-down self-esteem (much like an abused partner who won't leave). The child may secretly talk with the target about how bad it is. In at least one case, the blamer with antisocial tendencies was later arrested for an unrelated antisocial behavior, and custody was returned to the other parent, to the great relief of the child, who then refused to see the antisocial parent for over a year.

The best defense against such a postdivorce battle is to continue to keep records on parenting behavior and to have other people witness that the child is doing well with you. Sometimes photos or videotapes of good times together with you and the children help block new allegations. Also, discuss with your therapist whether your blamer's behavior patterns may suggest traits of an antisocial personality. If not, such a battle is less likely to occur.

## Maintaining Stability

Given these potential problems, try to provide as much stability as possible for the children and your ex-partner. Ease them into changes, rather than waiting until the last minute to surprise them. Be flexible and nonthreatening about schedule changes and involvement of relatives and new relationships. Avoid forcing a new partner into full and frequent contact with the children and your ex-partner. Gradual change is easier to take, especially for blamers, whose first reaction to almost everything is negative. If you're seeking a minor change in the parenting schedule or support payments, float the idea first in a casual conversation or through a third party to determine the blamer's state of mind before you take any action. Then weigh the costs (financial and emotional) of a court battle against the benefit of the modification. Suggest an out-of-court method of handling the issue, such as mediation or other negotiations.

## If You Have to Go to Court

If the blamer's behavior becomes extreme, you may have to go to court. More likely, the blamer will take you to court, and often by surprise. So keep an attorney in the wings for occasional checkups, and keep your records handy. You never know when you will need to do a quick declaration for a sudden emergency court hearing. Then, use the skills and knowledge (and documents) you gained from your prior divorce experience.

It's especially helpful to keep good quotes from transcripts of the evaluator's or judge's statements during the divorce. Since you may have a new judge by now, this can often help nip things in the bud. Submit a copy of the strongest words the former judge had for the blamer: "I am sanctioning you for bringing this totally meritless hearing before the court without a change of circumstances. If you bring such a meritless hearing again, I will sanction you again." When a new judge hears that, it may save hours of new court hearings.

You may have had a judge who completely misunderstood your case, made decisions influenced by the blamer's emotional persuasion, and refused to allow deeper evaluation of the case. In that case, you will need to gather better evidence before you have to go to court again. At least you will know what's in the court record, so that you can have facts to show to rebut false claims if they are brought up again. Many postdivorce hearings don't last long. Once it's clear that you're prepared and ready to take a very assertive approach again, some blamers back off.

But don't be surprised if the court starts over from scratch with your case. Most court counselors, attorneys, and judges are not trained in the family dynamics surrounding PDs. Instead, they have taken training in abuse dynamics, alienation dynamics, or other specific issues. So, regardless of the past, they may think of your case only in terms of the latest issue or theory they have been trained in and look for evidence proving or disproving that theory.

Often you will have new professionals—counselors, attorneys, evaluators, and judges—looking at your case and seeing only the surface issues at the beginning. The big picture of underlying PDs and postdivorce dynamics for blamers may never be considered. While it may seem as though you're starting over again as well, you now have much more knowledge of how the system works and what to do to protect yourself. If you're well prepared for the worst, you may never have to face these postdivorce scenarios.

## Conclusion

The postdivorce relationship generally needs to be managed in cases of a BP, NP, or ASP blamer. Some of the worst custody battles take place after the divorce. Enforcing court orders can be a major difficulty, but there are a variety of methods for dealing with this. On the other hand, you may find that you want or need to modify prior orders. There are also methods for dealing with this, as well as cautions when you are dealing with a blamer. Also, be prepared for your former partner to take you back to court, by practicing the methods described throughout this book, especially keeping good records of events.

Outside court, it is very important to find a stable balance in relating to your former partner: Avoid being too close or too rejecting. Avoid the common error of cutting the person off or trying to be really close friends. Both approaches can easily backfire. If you find a good balance, then managing the aftermath of your divorce may feel inconvenient at times, but it won't be the roller coaster of crisis and confrontation you may have experienced in the past.

*Chapter 17*

# Conclusion

Picture this courtroom scene. A man is called to testify, but he's totally drunk. He staggers to the witness stand, trips on the step, and falls on the witness chair, knocking it down. He gets up and points across the room: "It's all her fault," he slobbers. "She made me fall down. She's dangerous. She hurts me and our child. Don't ever—uh, you can't believe a thing she says."

Of course, the judge would excuse him and pay no attention to what he said. He was "under the influence," so confronting his actions or statements would be pointless—at least until he sobered up.

The problem for people with PDs is very similar, in that they are operating "under the influence" of constant cognitive distortions: exaggerated fears, all-or-nothing thinking, jumping to conclusions, emotional reasoning, and projecting. Yet they are not consciously aware that these are distortions. Instead, they believe their distortions and act on them. Unfortunately, legal professionals often believe the distortions and act on them as well. There is no obvious sign, such as appearing drunk, to disbelieve them. Instead, the blamers are very persuasive.

If you question blamers' thinking, they take it as a personal attack. It triggers a defensive survival response, which is usually to attack back. They try to protect themselves in ways that only make matters worse, through physical violence, verbal abuse, or false allegations. Even without feedback, they constantly feel as if their lives—and their children's lives—are in danger. They think they must fight back against forces that don't understand them or care about them: their targets of blame.

In divorce, you become the target. Blamers come to court, not intending to act badly and make false allegations, but to get help from those in authority to solve problems that make them feel hopeless, abandoned, and inferior. Unfortunately, when they enter today's family court culture, legal professionals may totally believe their concerns about being victims, taking them at face value as signs of abuse, because that is a top concern in many of today's family courts, as it should be.

This can result in targets being falsely accused of a wide range of abusive behavior, often resulting in punitive court orders limiting their healthy relationships with their children, controlling their incomes, excluding them from their property, and affecting their careers. On the other hand, targets may be accused of making false allegations of abuse, and the court may believe the blamer and fail to protect true victims or the children from future violence and other dangerous behavior.

Aggressively blaming the blamer isn't the solution either. Some family courts today totally disbelieve the blamer and publicly criticize the person for being stupid or crazy (neither of which is true) without any understanding of her underlying logic and fears. This doesn't help the target in the long run, because humiliating blamers in court simply triggers more cognitive distortions for them and more misbehavior outside court. Conflict often escalates with repeated hearings, more distortion campaigns against the target outside court, or both.

The best overall strategy for targets of blame is to take a very assertive approach: to quickly, and in a matter-of-fact way, provide credible, factual information to the court and to try to be as perfect as possible in every way during the court process.

By explaining the patterns of your blamer's behavior and organizing your information well, you can educate your attorney, therapist, evaluator, and judge about the underlying patterns of behavior in your case. But you can't rely on professionals to comprehend or even consider the concept of PDs. They may reject this idea out of hand as irrelevant or violating the no-fault divorce culture by "disparaging" someone's personality. So you must rely more on exposing the blamer's false statements and serious misbehaviors and on presenting accurate information about you in response to each major false allegation. Evidence and credibility win in the long run.

You must also develop good relationships. Hire a therapist as early as possible to discuss your own thoughts and feelings about the divorce and going to court. Talk about how your therapist can be helpful for you in the court process. Do sufficient research in hiring your attorney so that you won't have to change attorneys when the allegations get worse or if the court makes frustrating "just-to-be-safe" bad decisions at the beginning of your case.

Predict crises in your case based on common blamer behavior and discuss with your attorney the best way to handle them. Find out your attorney's preferences for communicating with you. Provide information that's thorough, but in a manner that's easiest for your attorney to use. Understand your attorney's schedule and how to work with it.

Approach your court-appointed evaluator as a friend, not an enemy. Organize your information and explain what's really happening. Now is not the time to hold back or "walk on eggshells." Disclose full factual information about your case. Provide information about the blamer's behaviors (who, what, when, and where) to your evaluator and explain how you think it might fit the dynamics of a personality problem in your case. Focus on explaining patterns of unchanging harmful behavior, and let the evaluator make a diagnosis. The label is less important than recognizing the patterns.

Remember, never tell others that you have diagnosed a PD in your partner, although you can tell your attorney you suspect this is true. You are not qualified to make a diagnosis, and telling others just escalates resistance to any cooperation whatsoever. We have seen this over and over again. Don't tell your partner that he has a PD! It will make your case and your life much more difficult, possibly for years to come. It triggers extreme defensiveness and resistance to any kind of reasonable settlement.

You may discuss "possible patterns" with a therapist or an evaluator, but let the evaluator make the diagnosis or explain the pattern to the court without giving it a name. The goal isn't to label someone with a disorder, but to understand (and have the court understand) the patterns of the person's behavior so that you can best protect yourself, if necessary, and reach a positive settlement, if possible.

Persuasive BP, NP, or ASP blamers are truly driven by the false alarms of their constant cognitive distortions. They physically, verbally, and legally abuse others in an effort to obtain power and control, because they chronically feel so out of control. While they lie and consciously manipulate at times, understand that their underlying intensity and distress are based on unconscious defense mechanisms. They may believe the false information they are saying and submitting to the court.

Others' disdain, lectures, and anger rarely motivate them. They need consequences and a program of change, such as batterer's treatment, substance-abuse treatment, skills training, ongoing therapy with a consistent therapist who understands their personality problems, or some combination of these solutions. Getting your blamer into therapy is neither likely nor your problem to solve. As your court case proceeds, expect crises, personal attacks, and a roller coaster of anger and desperate pleas for help from your blamer that you need to learn to manage or ignore.

Use your support system. Expect more allegations as you present more factual information. Don't burn out or give up, but be willing to let go of minor or irresolvable issues. Choose your battles with a long-term perspective. Many negative advocates drop out after they learn the facts about the blamer and after the battle tires them out. If you can remain assertive and consistent in protecting yourself over time, you may no longer be their target. But remember that the divorce doesn't end your relationship with your former partner who has BP, NP, or ASP tendencies. There is a high risk of future controversies and possible court hearings.

If you share parenting, develop a stable, arm's-length relationship that's neither too rejecting nor too intimate with your ex-partner. Support an appropriate relationship between your children and your ex so that she doesn't feel constantly threatened with feelings of loss or inferiority. Keep records of events that could be useful if you return to court.

Splitting up is never easy. The more you educate yourself, obtain support, avoid actions that make you a target, and take an assertive approach, the better off you will be on this difficult journey. Remember to KEEP CALM: develop knowledge and energy to assertively explain patterns of behavior, while considering alternatives to litigation and managing the postdivorce relationship.

Best wishes!

# Acknowledgments

We would like to acknowledge each other's work in the creation of the first and second editions of this book. For almost twenty years, this book has been a true collaboration, as we have shared with one another problems and solutions for people who have contacted us in need of this information. It has been a mutually rewarding experience.

Bill thanks his wife, Alice, who deserves extra credit for coping with his writing and seminar schedule for so many years in addition to his day job of handling divorces as a lawyer and mediator. Bill also thanks his clients, who have taught him the most by sharing their ups and downs and their insights and growth. Thanks go to Megan Hunter for her hard work and positive energy in cofounding and growing the High Conflict Institute beyond my wildest imagination.

Bill also wants to thank Gordon Cruse, CFLS, for his wisdom about electronically stored information in legal cases, and Bill Benjamin, CFLS, for his early mentoring and ongoing insights into the ethical and strategic practice of family law.

We want to thank the editors and design staff at New Harbinger Publications, particularly Jennye Garibaldi and Karen Levy for their guidance and detailed suggestions and Michele Waters for making this a more professional and user-friendly book that anyone can use. We also want to thank Scott Edelstein for his expert assistance in building our relationship with New Harbinger Publications.

# Resources

## High Conflict Institute LLC

Cofounded by Bill Eddy, LCSW, Esq., and Megan L. Hunter, MBA, the High Conflict Institute provides education and resources primarily to professionals handling high-conflict disputes, as well as to the general public. For live or video training, books, articles, and consultation, go to www.High ConflictInstitute.com or call (619) 800-2070. We also have a website for a wide range of conflict resolution self-help resources: www.ConflictPlaybook.com.

## New Ways for Families®

Developed by Bill Eddy and the High Conflict Institute, New Ways for Families® is a skills training method for parents going through separation and divorce. It is available as a short-term counseling method, as a live class, and as an online class with a coaching option. For more information, go to www.High ConflictInstitute.com or call (619) 800-2070.

## Co-author Randi Kreger's Website

www.BPDcentral.com

A website, bookstore, and online support group run by Randi Kreger, the co-author of this book. You can access the online support group, Moving Forward, from here.

Visit the companion webpage to this book at www.newharbin ger.com/46110 for more resources, including:

- Sample letters to professionals, family, and friends about what you may be going through and how to help in a separation and divorce

- Other books and resources by the authors

- Articles on related topics for individuals going through a separation or divorce

# References

American Psychiatric Association: *Diagnostic and Statistical Manual of Mental Disorders*. 5th ed. 2013. Arlington, VA, American Psychiatric Association.

American Psychiatric Association: *Diagnostic and Statistical Manual of Mental Disorders*. 4th ed. 1994. Arlington, VA: American Psychiatric Association, 1994.

Bancroft, L., and J. G. Silverman. 2002. *The Batterer as Parent: Addressing the Impact of Domestic Violence on Family Dynamics*. Thousand Oaks, CA: Sage Publications.

Beck, A. T., A. Freeman, and Associates. 1990. *Cognitive Therapy of Personality Disorders*. New York: The Guilford Press.

Carpenter, S. 2008. "Buried Prejudice: The Bigot in Your Brain." *Scientific American Mind* 19: 33–39.

Ceci, S. J., and M. Bruck. 1995. *Jeopardy in the Courtroom: A Scientific Analysis of Children's Testimony*. Washington, DC: American Psychological Association.

Dutton, D. G. 2007. *The Abusive Personality: Violence and Control in Intimate Relationships*. 2nd ed. New York: The Guilford Press.

Eddy, B. 2020. *Don't Alienate the Kids! Raising Resilient Children While Avoiding High Conflict Divorce*. 2nd ed. Scottsdale, AZ: Unhooked Books.

Eddy, B., A. T. Burns, and K. Chafin. 2020. *BIFF for CoParent Communication: Your Guide to Difficult CoParent Texts, Emails and Social Media Posts.* Scottsdale, AZ: Unhooked Books.

Eddy, B. 2016. *High Conflict People in Legal Disputes.* 2nd ed. Scottsdale, AZ: Unhooked Books.

Farrell, J. M., I. A. Shaw, and M. A. Webber. 2009. "A Schema-Focused Approach to Group Psychotherapy for Outpatients with Borderline Personality Disorder: A Randomized Controlled Trial." *Journal of Behavior Therapy and Experimental Psychiatry* 40: 317–28.

Fonagy, P., and P. Luyten. 2009. "A Developmental, Mentalization-Based Approach to the Understanding and Treatment of Borderline Personality Disorder." *Development and Psychopathology* 21: 1355–81.

Friedel, R. O. 2004. *Borderline Personality Disorder Demystified: An Essential Guide for Understanding and Living with BPD.* New York: Marlowe and Company.

———. 2006. Unpublished interview by Randi Kreger, April.

Goleman, D. 2006. *Social Intelligence: The New Science of Human Relationships.* New York: Bantam Dell.

Grant, B. F., S. P. Chou, R. B. Goldstein, B. Huang, F. S. Stinson, T. D. Saha, et al. 2008. "Prevalence, Correlates, Disability, and Comorbidity of DSM-IV Borderline Personality Disorder: Results from the Wave 2 National Epidemiologic Survey on Alcohol and Related Conditions." *Journal of Clinical Psychiatry* 69: 533–45.

Grant, B. F., D. S. Hasin, F. S. Stinson, D. A. Dawson, S. P. Chou, W. J. Ruan, and R. P. Pickering. 2004. "Prevalence, Correlates, and Disability of Personality Disorders in the United States: Results from the National Epidemiologic

Survey on Alcohol and Related Conditions." *Journal of Clinical Psychiatry* 65: 948–58.

Iacoboni, M. 2008. *Mirroring People: The New Science of How We Connect with Others*. New York: Farrar, Straus, and Giroux.

Johnston, J., V. Roseby, and K. Kuehnle. 2009. *In the Name of the Child: A Developmental Approach to Understanding and Helping Children of Conflicted and Violent Divorce*. New York: Springer Publishing Company.

Kelly, J. B., and M. P. Johnson. 2008. "Differentiation Among Types of Intimate Partner Violence: Research Update and Implications for Interventions." *Family Court Review* 46: 476–99.

Kreger, R. 2008. *The Essential Family Guide to Borderline Personality Disorder: New Tools and Techniques to Stop Walking on Eggshells*. Center City, MN: Hazelden.

Kübler-Ross, E. 1969. *On Death and Dying: What the Dying Have to Teach Doctors, Nurses, Clergy, and Their Own Families*. New York: Collier Books.

Lawson, C. A. 2002. *Understanding the Borderline Mother: Helping Her Children Transcend the Intense, Unpredictable, and Volatile Relationship*. Northvale, NJ: Jason Aronson.

Lewicki, R. J., B. Barry, and D. M. Saunders. 2010. *Negotiation*. 6th ed. Boston: Richard Irwin.

Linehan, M. M. 1993. *Cognitive-Behavioral Treatment of Borderline Personality Disorder*. New York: The Guilford Press.

Mason, P. T., and R. Kreger. 2010. *Stop Walking on Eggshells: Taking Your Life Back When Someone You Care About Has Borderline Personality Disorder*. 2nd ed. Oakland, CA: New Harbinger Publications.

Millon, T. 1996. *Disorders of Personality: DSM-IV and Beyond.* 2nd ed. With R. D. Davis. New York: John Wiley and Sons.

Rieke, R. D., and R. K. Stutman. 1990. *Communication in Legal Advocacy.* Columbia, SC: University of South Carolina Press.

Schore, A. N. 2003. *Affect Regulation and the Repair of the Self.* New York: W. W. Norton and Company.

Stinson, F. S., D. A. Dawson, R. B. Goldstein, S. P. Chou, B. Huang, S. M. Smith, et al. 2008. "Prevalence, Correlates, Disability, and Comorbidity of DSM-IV Narcissistic Personality Disorder: Results from the Wave 2 National Epidemiologic Survey on Alcohol and Related Conditions." *Journal of Clinical Psychiatry* 69: 1033–45.

Twenge, J. M., and W. K. Campbell. 2009. *The Narcissism Epidemic: Living in the Age of Entitlement.* New York: Free Press.

Wallin, D. J. 2007. *Attachment in Psychotherapy.* New York: The Guilford Press.

Young, J. E., J. S. Klosko, and M. E. Weishaar. 2003. *Schema Therapy: A Practitioner's Guide.* New York: The Guilford Press.

**Bill Eddy, LCSW, JD,** is a family lawyer, therapist, and mediator in San Diego, CA. He is cofounder and chief innovation officer at High Conflict Institute, and trains lawyers, judges, mediators, and counselors worldwide in respectfully managing high-conflict disputes and personalities. He is author of sixteen books, developer of the *New Ways for Families*® method for separation and divorce, and blogger for *Psychology Today* with more than five million views. His website is www.highconflict institute.com.

**Randi Kreger** is author of three books about borderline personality disorder (BPD), including *Stop Walking on Eggshells.* She is creator of www.StopWalkingOnEggshells.com; and runs the online support group, Moving Forward. She publishes specialized CDs and other materials about BPD, which are available on her website.

# MORE BOOKS from
# NEW HARBINGER PUBLICATIONS

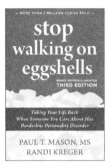

Register your **new harbinger** titles for additional benefits!

When you register your **new harbinger** title—purchased in any format, from any source—you get access to benefits like the following:

- Downloadable accessories like printable worksheets and extra content
- Instructional videos and audio files
- Information about updates, corrections, and new editions

Not every title has accessories, but we're adding new material all the time.

Access free accessories in 3 easy steps:

**1.** Sign in at NewHarbinger.com (or **register** to create an account).

**2.** Click on **register a book**. Search for your title and click the **register** button when it appears.

**3.** Click on the **book cover or title** to go to its details page. Click on **accessories** to view and access files.

That's all there is to it!

If you need help, visit:

NewHarbinger.com/accessories

**new harbinger**
CELEBRATING
**40** YEARS